TRANSFORMATIVE STUDENT VOICE

TRANSFORMATIVE

STUDENT

VOICE

PARTNERING WITH YOUNG PEOPLE FOR EQUITABLE SCHOOL IMPROVEMENT

Shelley Zion, Ben Kirshner, and
Carlos P. Hipolito-Delgado

HARVARD EDUCATION PRESS
Cambridge, Massachusetts

Paperback ISBN 9781682539828
Library of Congress Cataloging-in-Publication Data is on file.

Published by Harvard Education Press,
an imprint of the Harvard Education Publishing Group

Harvard Education Press
8 Story Street
Cambridge, MA 02138

Cover Design: Endpaper Studio

The typefaces in this book are Latienne, Agenda, and Avenir Next.

Dedication

First and foremost, we dedicate this book to the youth activists and the adults who make space for them: educators and coaches, teachers and counselors, principals and superintendents, community organizers and families.

Shelley: For my daughters, Jasmine and Jamica, who were the first (and best) participants (and teachers) in my effort to share power and voice with young people. In the memory of my Grandma Rhea, who showed me how to be an activist and use my voice. And to my husband, Delano, who shares my curiosity, protects my peace, and holds me accountable to our shared vision.

Ben: To my son, Jackson, whose generosity of spirit, insight, and humor keeps me growing and learning. To Elizabeth, whose grace, compassion, and love for the world inspires me.

Carlos: Para Meztli y Joaquin, you are my wildest dreams come true. For my Mom, thank you for all your sacrifices and for teaching me the importance of education. For Emma, Ricky, and Hector, you continue to be my role models. To Abby, thank you for being my partner, proofreader, external reviewer, consultant, support system, and source of love.

Contents

Foreword by Solicia Ester Lopez   ix

SECTION 1   The What, Why, and How of
Transformative Student Voice   1

ONE   What Is Transformative Student Voice?   5

TWO   Getting Ready   33

THREE   School Improvement Planning
and School Reform   51

SECTION 2   TSV Implementation   71

FOUR   At the District Level   75

FIVE   In the Classroom and Curriculum
(with Dane Stickney)   103

SIX   Afterschool Clubs, Summer Sessions,
and Professional Development   131

SECTION 3   Bringing It All Together   151

SEVEN   When Voice Becomes Activism   153

EIGHT   Conclusion   171

*Appendix A: Evidence of Student
Voice Impacts*   191

Appendix B: Building Your Team   195

Notes   199

Acknowledgments   219

About the Authors   221

Index   225

Foreword

Every day I am dedicated to serving my people and community as an activist educator. My journey to this point has been shaped by my identity and experiences as a Native American woman, daughter, granddaughter, niece, sister, mother, grandmother, auntie, femtor, and friend, as well as my deep roots in my community. Born and raised in the Westwood neighborhood, and a third-generation Colorado native, I've seen firsthand the importance of creating spaces where voices—especially those historically marginalized—are not just heard, but empowered to ignite real change. My work has always been about fostering youth-adult partnerships and strategic initiatives that uplift young people and their communities. I've dedicated my career to equipping students with the knowledge and confidence to advocate for their needs, while helping them understand the larger systems that shape their experiences.

Transformative Student Voice: Partnering with Young People for Equitable School Improvement is a resource I wish I'd had to guide me when I was designing and implementing the successful grassroots organizing student voice and leadership model that I led and grew to twenty-plus high schools. Having this book as a "how to" would have helped me avoid unnecessary challenges when navigating the politics of schools and administration. Grounded in research and years of practice, it offers practical strategies for district administrators—whether leading large urban systems or smaller rural districts—to foster and sustain Transformative Student Voice at every level of decision-making.

My research practice partnership with Shelley Zion, Carlos Hipolito-Delgado, and Ben Kirshner was instrumental in demonstrating that when students are given the opportunity to lead in partnership with adults, they drive their own learning and gain the knowledge and ability to transform school and district policies and systems. This book shows that when students are given the opportunity to lead, they become powerful agents of change—not only in their learning but in the systems that shape their learning experiences and futures.

Student voice is key to unlocking both transformational student learning and systems-level change. For district administrators and those in training, this book addresses the *why* and the *how*. Why? Because marginalized students in particular bring critical perspectives that can guide us toward more equity-centered solutions. Their lived experiences, ideas, and leadership are essential in pushing us to create systems that work for all learners. Their beautiful and precious knowledge sheds light on the real barriers to learning, and their solutions often surpass the expectations of adults in the system.

This book also addresses the *how* by providing strategies drawn from diverse districts across the country, offering examples of how to create systems that equip students to transform their learning environments. These approaches are designed to elevate the voices that matter most and create thriving school communities where all students can grow intellectually and emotionally.

Moreover, the strategies outlined in this book offer a pathway for creating *sustainable* structures that elevate student perspectives and ensure those voices are heard, respected, and, most importantly, acted upon. This is not just about listening—it's about transforming our schools to reflect the dreams and aspirations of our students and their families. When young people feel heard, valued, and respected in their learning environments the outcomes typically lead to success in all elements of their lives.

These ideas are at the center of my attention now, as I embrace a new phase of my leadership in a new district department that merges family and community engagement with student voice and leadership. This department will be more than a structural realignment—it is a pioneering initiative aimed at ensuring that the aspirations and needs of students and their families are central to every decision the district makes. I find the chapters in this book useful as I explore different parts of youth engagement, both formal opportunities for voice but also how to build on the insights of student activists and agitators fighting for a better world.

As you read, I encourage you to think deeply about how you can use student voice to inform your leadership approach, strategies, and actions. In doing so, you'll not only transform your district—you'll empower students to become bold learners, leaders, and activists for a stronger future. Reflect on how you can center student voice in your leadership, not just as an initiative, but as a guiding principle for building a more just and informed school system.

Remember, the question isn't only why we should make student voices central to our work, but *how to do it in high quality, equitable, and sustainable ways.*

Solicia Ester Lopez,
Chicana/Indigenous—
Spiritually Raised Lakota

The What, Why, and How of Transformative Student Voice

THIS SECTION INCLUDES THREE CHAPTERS that will help you understand what Transformative Student Voice is (and is *not*), and why you should work to integrate Transformative Student Voice (TSV) into your educational system—from the district, to the school, to the classroom, and also outward into the community. We'll lay out the details of how to get started, build your team, and develop the structures that ensure success.

In chapter 1, we define TSV, explore its four key elements, and make the distinction between *transformative* student voice and forms of student voice that are about input or choice. We also discuss the *why*—from our own research as well as the larger body of research literature. And we will dig into the challenges of schools today, addressing issues of racial justice, gender inequality, and LGBTQIA+ inclusion, and identifying barriers to access for students identified as dis/abled or poor, or those for whom English is not their native language. We take up the tension between centering student voice because it is the moral or just thing to do, and the pragmatic possibilities of using student voice as a lever to motivate increased engagement with school, improved compliance with behavioral expectations, and increased academic achievement—all important factors that influence leadership decisions.

In chapter 2, we get practical. We discuss our model for vertical and horizontal integration and the infrastructure needed to support implementation. We identify the places in an organization where student voice should be centered, and we discuss how to revise policy and practice to ensure that students are centered in educator hiring and evaluation, curriculum and pedagogical practices, teacher professional development, school improvement and planning processes, and policymaking spaces. We follow this with some strategies to help leaders determine the *how* that works for their district or school, including where to start, how to set the stage, how to identify the right team members (teacher-leaders, administrators, and students) to get started, how to craft the best structures, and what resources you will need. We discuss the necessary dispositions, the mindset shifts that must happen, the skills that need to be developed (for both adults and youth), and the challenges to anticipate when committing to what is both a process and a goal. We identify current schooling structures that are likely to be barriers to full implementation and discuss how to navigate those barriers. We will highlight our "lessons learned" in the form of missteps to avoid, and we will support leaders in connecting this work to learning standards, school improvement processes, and other district-specific strategic plans, goals, or initiatives. By the end of the chapter, you will have a plan for building a team, getting stakeholder buy-in, and communicating the strategy to the larger community.

In chapter 3, we focus on how to engage students in whole-school improvement, reform, and transformation. We outline a clear strategy to develop authentic youth-adult partnerships that center the voices of students in school improvement efforts and include them as authentic partners in climate transformation, policy development, classroom design, pedagogy, professional development, curriculum development, hiring and evaluation, and annual school performance reports. We use data from a four-year project with a large urban school district to highlight the challenges inherent in working to shift the mindsets of adults to equip them to share power with young people. We will share additional stories (both successful and less so) of how young people have been included in these processes at the school and district levels; how their participation helped ensure relevant content, powerful learning experiences, and reductions in discipline and bullying; and how they helped to build real buy-in from key stakeholders—the students themselves. As we share these stories, we will point out the strategies that work, from the basics of allowing for plenty of time and scheduling meetings at times when young people can participate, to learning how to ask questions, take up multiple perspectives, uncover the values that drive positions, communicate across differences, call people in, and map power relationships. We'll also identify the key skills needed—for young people and adults—to contribute to these collaborations. All educational leaders know that engaging stakeholders is key, and that students are important stakeholders, but leaders often don't know where to start or what changes to implement.

ONE

What Is Transformative Student Voice?

WHAT DO YOU SEE ON THE WALLS of your school building, the district website, or in your school's key documents? Do the daily actions of the faculty, staff, and administration live up to the challenges laid out in your mission, vision, or values statement? Are you ready to make those words a reality? In schools across the country, we see brightly colored signs that read:

Put each student first, every day.

Our mission is to educate students for success in a changing world.

Through its educational alliances, [the district] will empower all students to become successful, productive, life-long learners.[1]

Building tomorrow's leaders today.[2]

Our vision is to ensure that all students receive an outstanding education, maximize their potential, and demonstrate responsible citizenship in the community and on our planet.

This environment will enable all to develop fully the academic, emotional, social and physical potential, and thus be empowered to assume responsible citizenship in our local, national, and global communities.[3]

School mission statements, created to establish a shared purpose and to guide the direction of decision-makers, often make lofty claims about prioritizing young people, preparing students for success in a changing world, and empowering youth to be engaged citizens.[*] In a 2013 study, Schafft and Biddle noted that *lifelong learning*, *preparing students for a global society*, and *creating productive citizens* are phrases present in the vast majority of district mission statements.[4] In our work with school and district leaders we rarely encounter objections to the idea that "student voices matter" or "we value student voice." Such ideas—that we should learn from student experience, that students should learn to be citizens, that student leadership is important—are ubiquitous.

And yet . . . Scratch the surface and one finds either no enactment of these ideas or implementation that is so superficial or circumscribed as to be almost meaningless. The experiences and perspectives of students, and their perceptions of school and learning, are rarely centered in education policy, practice, and research.[5] The research literature has clearly documented that the voices of students are rarely heard in debates about schooling and school reform.[6] When schools do include students in school policy and reform conversations, it is most often in ways that are tokenistic—completing surveys

---

[*] Note that we vary our word choice in talking about students, youth, or young people—although our focus is on transformative *student* voice, we acknowledge that this work often occurs in out-of-school settings.

or making choices between preselected options—and focus on those students already identified as "leaders," namely, those who are engaged, successful, and compliant.[7]

This contradiction, between the rhetoric of student voice and the reality of business as usual, leaves us, as educators and school or district leaders, not only failing to meet the goals of the mission statements that guide us, but also working without the viewpoints of the people we claim to serve, which goes against everything we know about how changes stick.

In this chapter, we introduce the evidence about how we can design, implement, and sustain school transformation efforts by focusing on the critical element of *including all stakeholders*—especially those who are the intended beneficiaries of those changes. We'll then lay out the evidence of why our approach, Transformative Student Voice (TSV), supports the varied goals and intentions of school mission statements and helps us transform schools in sustainable ways. We'll delve deeper into the key elements of TSV, discuss some of the challenges of implementing it, and discuss things that look like, but are not, TSV. We'll follow that with a chapter on how to get ready, and then share six chapters that each take up an in-depth discussion of different ways that TSV can happen—with cases and examples to guide your work.

WHAT DO WE KNOW ABOUT SCHOOL REFORM?

The language of public policy and research has used the framing of *school reform* as a way to talk about changes meant to improve schooling. However, a new generation of educators and researchers has shifted to the notion of *school transformation*, to shift from making changes within the existing system to challenging the logic, purpose, and structure of the existing system. In this book, we'll use both—because sometimes our work is about making smaller changes within the existing system, and sometimes it's about larger or more structural changes. It's why we call our intervention *transformative* student voice—because centering students, as partners with adults, is a structural change.

MERCEDES SOSA, DIRECTOR OF YOUTH LEADERSHIP, URBAN SCHOOL DISTRICT (USD)

 And I think also trying to help our young people think about, in terms of policy isn't easy work. It could be very slow, and that many, many times, it will look like it's almost a sense of defeat or it's not going anywhere. But you have to continue to put in the work.

(Throughout the book, we use pseudonyms to refer to all people and places, other than our research team, so as to protect the anonymity of participants in research.)

Sustaining change requires that every area of the system shifts in the desired direction. It must include an evolution of mindsets about the system, with a process driven by the needs of the people served by the system; it must be based on the beliefs and values of those people; and it must incorporate a shared vision.[8] A critical tension in this work is to identify who is served by the system. Are the interests we focus on those of our democracy? Of the workforce? Or of the students themselves? If we return to the mission statements quoted in the opening of this chapter, it appears that schools claim students as the intended beneficiaries of the system, and thus should build their vision and strategy for change based on the needs of young people; grounded in their beliefs, values, and experiences; and developed via a process of shared visioning. It is these goals that have led us to the development of Transformative Student Voice, and the remainder of the book will help you develop the structures to shift the system—and adult mindsets—toward building authentic youth-adult partnerships, creating a place at the table for young people to lead us in our vision of better educational systems.

THE PROBLEM WITH SCHOOL "IMPROVEMENT" AND "REFORM"

School improvement work tends to focus on programs—literacy and math, or character education and PBIS (Positive Behavior Interventions and Supports)—with more progressive districts leaning into trauma-informed, restorative, and culturally responsive practices. All of these programs are designed by adults to "fix" issues with student learning and behavior, as identified by adults. But in our twenty years of doing research projects with students, when asked to identify the issues that matter to them, the young people tend to focus on issues of belonging, respect, and voice. They want more choices, and they want to be heard. They want to be confident that if and when they experience microaggressions or implicit bias, those issues will be addressed. They want adults who will talk to them, listen to them, and value them. Data from our partner districts over the past three years show that 46 percent of TSV projects focused on issues of equity and diversity, 30 percent focused on including student voice in various policy or leadership processes, and 13 percent focused on issues related to student health and wellness.

Our argument for the centering of students in school reform work is grounded in a visionary pragmatism, which balances the pragmatic need to work within the system with the visionary ideals of empowerment and emancipation.[9] School reform models appeal to the logic of educators, policymakers, and reformers, and we draw on those in our work, but also on the more emancipatory ideas of Paulo Freire, who named the potential for education to be "the practice of freedom, the means by which men and women deal critically and creatively with reality and discover how to participate in the transformation of their world."[10] We also draw on the systems design work of Béla Bánáthy, who focuses on the transformational and empowering potential of design work that centers the people impacted by the system:

> [E]ven if people fully develop their potential, they cannot give direction to their lives, they cannot forge their destiny, they cannot take charge of their future—unless they also develop the competence to take part directly and authentically in the design of the systems in which they live and work, and reclaim their right to do so. This is what true empowerment is about.[11]

Creating the space for young people to authentically engage in school reform requires learning and development on several fronts. Students need to develop the capacity to navigate school and life as critically conscious individuals and citizens. We also need to develop the knowledge and skills of adults to understand the impact of culture on our values, beliefs, and behaviors, and to engage in authentic youth-adult partnerships to transform schools.[12]

INTRODUCING THE WORK OF TRANSFORMATIVE STUDENT VOICE

We started this work together in 2008. Although we each followed our own paths to this work, with Shelley trained in critical theories of urban education and school reform, Carlos in school counseling, and Ben in youth development, we shared a foundational view that equity-focused school reform ought to be centered in student perspectives, experiences, and dreams for the future, with particular emphasis on those most marginalized by current systems.[13] At the time, we saw an important distinction between approaches to student voice that leaned more toward system maintenance as opposed to those focusing on system change.[14] System maintenance approaches tend to elevate the views of high-achieving students and restrict the topics that students can weigh in on. Not for us. System change approaches, in contrast, are anchored in anti-racist education principles, emphasize critical consciousness as a central aim of student leadership development, and draw on Youth Participatory Action Research (YPAR) as a core activity.

Critical consciousness, developed by Paulo Freire, is an educational aim that includes—but goes far beyond—the mastery of academic disciplines.[15] For Freire, the process of education is political, insofar as it typically socializes the learner into accepting and treating as "natural" existing inequalities and patterns of oppression. To counter this, education needs to be anchored in a problem-posing method that raises questions, unsettles dominant narratives, and awakens people to new visions for how they can live together. Rather than view discrimination, inequality, or police violence as part of the natural course of human social organization, critical consciousness pushes us to see such injustices as human-made and therefore changeable.

Critical consciousness is closely tied to YPAR, which also has roots in South America and revolutionary movements for social justice.[16] In YPAR, students select the topics of interest and produce original research that sheds light on issues that matter to them. Although YPAR may prioritize different ends depending on the context, projects share a commitment to centering young people's lived experience, making decisions as a collective, and engaging in a cycle that includes critical reflection, systematic research, and activism in the public sphere.[17] In these ways, YPAR offers a promising strategy for holding schools accountable for being more just, equitable, and culturally responsive to youth.[18] Because of its social change aims, YPAR has tended to be more common in

community programs, university-based projects, and sometimes school elective classes, rather than in K–12 academic
courses.[19]

Although opportunities for critical consciousness and
YPAR are rare in public schools, several studies have reported
higher levels of academic engagement and learning for students who are part of such programs.[20] Students who have
previously felt alienated or marginalized from conventional
schooling begin to see how core academic practices can be a
vehicle for personal identity and community uplift. Engaging
in the cycles of action found in YPAR and action civics can contribute to or be a protective factor for student engagement,
agency, and belonging.[21]

Our interest in critical pedagogies, however, was not
merely because they foster student learning. YPAR is not just
a means to higher college-going rates or test scores. Critical
pedagogies are transformative because of their potential to
spur systemic change in schools and districts.

To get started, in 2008 we partnered with secondary
school classroom teachers to implement an approach we
called Critical Civic Inquiry (CCI). *Critical* refers to the idea
that students unearth, name, and problematize everyday
injustices or barriers to their dreams. *Civic* refers to its focus
on school or community improvement, though we emphasize that this curriculum is not limited to civics class. And we
use *inquiry* because the curriculum is centered on participatory action research, in which students study a phenomenon
anchored in their lived experience. CCI centers the life experiences, funds of knowledge, and aspirations of youth of
color from low-income communities, while also creating
opportunities that expand their knowledge and skills as leaders and agents of change.[22]

Our research about student learning and engagement in
the first phase of CCI projects provided evidence that participation in CCI could be a protective factor for ethnic identity,

academic engagement, and civic efficacy.[23] Qualitative case studies showed the ways in which skillful and persistent teachers facilitated opportunities for students to discuss racism and xenophobia and how their schools could become safer and more welcoming places. Students demonstrated new forms of leadership and voice in their efforts to transform their schools, such as by improving advising and school climate for undocumented students, countering racism and xenophobia toward Mexican American students by white students, and developing new workshops and policies to prevent bullying.

Our critical look at this work, however, also showed its limits for sustaining actual structural changes at the schools, in part because teachers were working in isolation. One teacher wrote that by teaching CCI she felt she was "going rogue" at her school, while others talked about feeling at odds with the norms and practices at their schools.[24] Several felt that facilitating a YPAR project called for far more work than just teaching their "regular curriculum." Many aspects of these challenges were structural, due to a lack of alignment between these programs and high-stakes testing or school governance policies.

This combination of findings—the evidence of student empowerment and the limitations of a fragmented approach—led us to embrace a more ambitious and systemic commitment to student voice, one not just situated in the classroom but in a variety of policies and practices. To get started, we explored what it would look like to scale CCI throughout a whole school or a whole district. We knew that even the best classroom work would be episodic and less impactful if it depended on the courageous work of isolated teachers, so we decided to explore a variety of more systemic approaches, including how to scale CCI through a whole school or enhance student voice across whole districts. We also realized that we needed to look at more than just classroom activities and should also include student roles in school leadership and feed-back loops—in brief, Transformative Student Voice. The rest of this book shares lessons and ideas from that journey.

THE *WHY*

For some, centering student voice is the moral or just thing to do; others lean into the pragmatic possibilities of using student voice as a lever to motivate increased engagement with school, improved compliance with behavioral expectations, and increased academic achievement. As we've already said, students, as key stakeholders and beneficiaries of the school system, should be included in school reform if we want changes to take hold. So ensuring the success of our reform initiatives is a definite *why*.

Another compelling *why* is that adults may not, in fact, know what is best for today's students. Not only are teachers still predominantly white, female, and middle class, while student demographics have become more diverse, educators tend to have historical perspectives about teaching and learning—many were successful in school, and so believe that it works as it is. But we also must acknowledge that the changing world means that what worked to prepare us for adulthood may very well not work for young people now. And who is a better source of information on the hopes and aspirations of today's youth than the youth themselves?

Schools have long claimed that a core purpose of schooling is to prepare students to be productive citizens in our democracy, and student voice work is a hands-on approach to developing the skills necessary to do so. This is especially urgent in a moment when core rights and democratic practices are under threat.

From a purely pragmatic perspective, schools have the charge of increasing the academic and social-emotional skills of young people. Student voice initiatives contribute to the development of so many of these: traditional academic and vocational skills; social, cultural, and interpersonal skills, including self-awareness and cultural proficiency in engaging with youth and adults from different demographic backgrounds; moral skills, which include deep reflection about one's individual choices and consequences and how these choices are impacted by broader social and historical circumstances; both basic and advanced civic and organizing skills; skills that support educational reform agendas, such as problem definition, data analysis, proposal writing, team work, strategy development, and public communication; and skills for effective partnering between youth and adults.[25]

WHAT IS TSV?

MS. MEADOW BLACKWELL, PRINCIPAL, JOHN LEWIS HIGH SCHOOL

 Our student voice team are the leaders amongst leaders. They are the students that I can see as true politicians, the students that are going to push the envelope. They're going to grow up to be the adults that are going to push for change in the community and in the world. They are the change that we expect to see. They are the leaders amongst our leaders.

TSV stands for the effort to create "sustained and systemic opportunities for students to inquire about the root causes of problems in their schools and take action to address them by working with adults to develop and implement better policies and practices."[26] Our approach to TSV is grounded in over fifteen years of research in urban, suburban, and rural schools and districts that center students in school and community reform, as well as with youth and community activist groups. We have a fifteen-year partnership with Urban School District

(USD)—a district of ninety thousand students in the western region of the US. We have other partnerships with a dozen small school districts—ranging in size from one thousand to eight thousand students—some rural, some suburban, and some urban-adjacent on the East Coast. We've also partnered with student voice projects on the West Coast and in the Southwest and the Midwest. We've worked with students as young as fourth grade, although our primary focus is at the middle and high school levels. We've done the work in classrooms, afterschool clubs, and summer programs.

So, what is TSV? We describe it as a process where, through youth-adult partnership, the voices of young people are centered in conversations about school and community improvement, and adults and youth develop a critical consciousness and capacity for engagement in sociopolitical action that results in a transformation of themselves and the settings where they live and work. We pay particular attention to the strategies needed to ensure that the role of student voice is not relegated to individual classrooms or projects nor limited to

FIGURE 1.1   **Classic word cloud**

input on surveys or choices preselected by adults, but is integrated into the daily work of the district and school.

It might be at this point that you feel yourself resisting a little: *But students can't have a voice in budgets, or curriculum, or hiring, or teacher evaluation!*

The image in figure 1.1 shows a range of places that student voice could and should be included—look at the options and identify those places you think student voice is, or could be, or should not be included. Then we challenge you to sit with that discomfort and imagine the ways they could.

KEY ELEMENTS OF TSV

There are five key elements of TSV that, when implemented, create a structure to center students in school reform and transformation and to maintain that centering over time. The five elements are: *sustained and systemic opportunities* for students to *inquire about the root causes of problems* in their schools and *take action to address them* by *working with adults* to *develop and implement better policies and practices.* Sounds good, but what does that mean?

Sustained and Systemic Opportunities

We must move away from onetime projects or classes and limited opportunities like surveys or focus groups and require that district and school leaders create intentional, ongoing structures for student engagement in inquiry. We'll discuss this in greater depth in the following chapters, but these might include embedding the key elements of TSV in core curriculum, creating afterschool clubs for TSV, or creating a TSV team supported by school administration. For example, USD's commitment to sustained and systemic student voice led them to create a dedicated program for promoting student voice in the district. They also hired staff to develop programming and support the implementation of student voice in district high schools. In South Country School District, leadership created an after-school and summer student voice program to embed TSV in district decision-making.

Inquire About the Root Causes of Problems

The shift from merely voicing complaints to collecting data that explores a range of perspectives and gets to the root causes of issues is what allows us to design solutions that will solve the problems that impact us rather than treat the symptoms. At USD's Southwest High School, students wanted to understand why their school had a poor performance rating with both the district and the state. They worked with school district officials, who explained that poor standardized test scores were to blame. The students then interviewed their peers about their experience taking standardized tests. Almost all of them related negative experiences with testing, but many described other features of the school, such as its diversity and student-teacher relationships, that they valued. But those features were not recognized because of the emphasis placed on test scores. The youth used those findings to lobby the district and state to reduce the weight of standardized testing in school ratings.

Take Action to Address Problems

Taking action requires that we use the data gathered to propose solutions—and to propose solutions that are actionable and doable. This element pushes young people and adults to grapple with the complexity of education systems and learn more about the various perspectives, possibilities, and obstacles to change. When pregnant and lactating mothers at Generations High School (in USD) realized that school lunches didn't meet their caloric needs, they proposed a policy to district officials to offer not only more nutritious but also more culturally diverse school food. After brief negotiations, the district agreed to meet most of their needs.

Work with Adults

Too often, students do projects, present them, get a grade, and move on to the next class. Alternatively, students raise an issue, make some demands, maybe stage a protest or walk out, and adults respond. In the TSV model, adults must partner with youth to create sustained and systemic opportunities, to engage in inquiry, and to take action. We have seen the TSV process facilitate meaningful relationships between high school students and district curriculum officials. At Urban Arts Academy (in USD), youth reported issues with consent and sexual safety. They asked the district to develop and offer a comprehensive health class. While the district was already planning on doing something similar, the health curriculum specialist asked the students to vet the developing curriculum, and she even implemented their revision ideas, including adding a youth research and action component as a summative assessment for the course.

Develop and Implement Better Policies and Practices

This is the outcome of the proceeding elements of the process—policies and practices that are informed by inquiry, devised in partnership between youth and adults, and create real possibility for lasting and meaningful change. While we have dozens of examples, one was surprisingly simple and powerful. Youth at the Justice School reported that the lack of free menstruation products was causing students stress. Neither the school nor their parents, the students said, seemed to want to engage in this issue. They instead forged a partnership with Planned Parenthood, who provided free menstruation products and educational materials, both of which can now be found in menstruation stations in the school's bathrooms.

TSV MINDSETS

The previous section laid out the structures and practices that embody TSV. Through our earlier work we've learned that the shift to new structures needs to be accompanied by a culture change among all the people who walk the school building: administrators, support staff, teachers, and students. Culture change, for us, means shifting people's mindsets—their mental models—for the work. The concepts we have to engage with, in order to implement those elements, follow.

Youth-Adult Partnerships

In a shift toward TSV, it is fundamental for school actors— whether students, teachers, or administrators—to embrace a *partnership* mindset. This is not easy. It requires unlearning traditional assumptions about the role of the teacher vis-à-vis the student. Adult assumptions about students' interest and engagement in school policy and practice, a fear of student critique, and the realities of systems of evaluation and accountability challenge our ability to create meaningful youth-adult partnerships.[27] It is also challenging because of generations of age segregation in schools, where students are placed in narrow age bands, organized by grade, and separated from collaborative opportunities with adults.[28]

The partnership mindset goes beyond just being a kind or caring teacher or school leader. Such qualities are necessary but not sufficient. After all, a kind or caring teacher might act in ways that are excessively paternalistic or adopt a "savior" mindset toward teenage youth, thinking, "I know what's right for you" or "I want to protect you from difficult conversations." Instead, the partnership mindset treats students as legitimate stakeholders and actors in decision-making processes; it looks for the kinds of expertise that students bring to planning and decision-making and does not treat age as a barrier to participation.[29]

The literature about youth development, often anchored in community spaces, has developed compelling frameworks to define youth-adult partnerships. A recent review defined youth-adult partnerships as:

> the practice of: (a) multiple youth and multiple adults deliberating and acting together, (b) in a collective [democratic] fashion (c) over a sustained period of time, (d) through shared work, (e) intended to promote social justice, strengthen an organization and/or affirmatively address a community issue.[30]

In this review, Shepherd Zeldin and colleagues cite examples of partnerships, often housed within city government, that have contributed to sustained youth participation in local governance or community planning.[31] Careful attention to these change efforts—both where they succeed and where they fail—has yielded a confident set of characterizations about youth-adult partnerships, which we apply to the school reform context.

Student-teacher partnerships require a major mental shift and a willingness to be vulnerable.[32] Effective youth-adult partnerships require that both educators and young people have the space and support to reflect on their own experiences, develop mutual respect and regard for each other, commit to supporting each other, and develop the skills required to work together to deconstruct the systemic barriers to building relationships and dismantling oppressive structures, while creating opportunities for youth to see themselves as powerful change agents and create the context for organizational and community change.[33]

This shift is not just one that adults need to make. Students, too, through the many years of schooling they've experienced, are not accustomed to working in collegial ways with adults. This can show up initially as passivity or reluctance to engage, especially in school contexts where students have had teachers who tell them what to do and when to learn. Novice teachers may be surprised to confront blank faces after their initial efforts to invite student choice or critical discussion. It may take time before youth really trust that the invitation is genuine. Skilled facilitation and scaffolding, in ways that engage all learners and recognize the funds of knowledge of students from minoritized backgrounds, is key.

We have also seen youth activist groups that are skeptical of working in partnership with adults. Some groups are so committed to youth-led or student-led actions and their age-based political identity that they restrict adults from contributing to strategy or decision-making. These kinds of student-led movements are exciting—we need more of them. But the model we describe here for transformative school change is different. Without adult buy-in, student empowerment and activism may take place in spaces distant from the machinery of actual power and without access to those responsible for enacting new policies and practices.

Sociopolitical Development

Our work on sociopolitical development and skills to take action builds on Roderick Watts's foundational work creating a five-stage model of sociopolitical development (SPD), which supports both students and teachers in developing "knowledge, analytical skills, emotional faculties, and capacity for action in political and social systems, while emphasizing an understanding of the cultural and political forces that shape one's status in society."[34] SPD is a process that does not exist solely within an individual, but in their activism within their community and toward the systems that create oppressive conditions.[35] Our work is not to "fix" students, but to create the conditions in which adults and young people explore their identities, learn from their experiences, and partner to challenge the systems that are not designed to support them. One of our first big learnings in the initial year of our work together was that we needed to spend as much time on ensuring the sociopolitical development of educators as we did on students. Most adults have not been supported in engaging in critical reflection on their own identities, positioning, and participation in systems of power and privilege, nor have we prepared educators to bring a critical lens to the historical, institutional, and structural legacies that influence opportunities and access. Adults must do this work with and alongside young people.

Systems Design

Our approach to this work utilizes systems design frameworks, which "enable designers to transcend the existing system, establish boundaries of design inquiry, and create some major design options of a desired future system."[36] This work is complicated by the challenges inherent in creating large-scale change; both humans and systems resist change, and equity-focused change confronts not just technical barriers, but also normative and political ones.[37] In systems design work, instead of accepting that the system as it is needs minor changes, we focus on what the system ought to be. For us, this begins with the radical notion that students should be centered in decision-making about policy and practices in their school settings. Further, building on the work of Charles Reigeluth and more recent calls for human-centered design, we build our interventions around a conceptual framework for successful systemic change—shown to be effective in whole-school change—in which partners focus on building broad stakeholder ownership with students as central stakeholders, committing to becoming learning organizations with an evolving mindset about what education systems can and should be, and developing an understanding of systems design and change processes in education settings.[38]

Youth at the Center

Within this broader systems design approach, the signature innovation we bring is to center young people—their lived experience, their dreams, their complexities—in design processes. This requires that schools ensure that there is dedicated time and space for students (in the classroom and on leadership teams) to learn together, do research, develop policy proposals, and share their work with school and district personnel; that student participants are reflective of the diversity of each school community, with priority given to recruiting and retaining students who are struggling or least-served by the current system; that all stakeholders are committed to leaning in to critical conversations about power and privilege, identity, and systems of oppression; and that students and teachers participate in learning and skill development in three areas: youth-adult partnerships, educational equity, and participatory action research.[39]

DR. SEAN OVERTON, SUPERINTENDENT, OAK KNOLL SCHOOL DISTRICT

 In terms of student voice, I think the biggest challenge or difference is the difference between true student voice and just student feedback. A lot of the schools are really at that level of getting student feedback and input, but in terms of the students actually driving change, I think they're worried . . . that, in general, teachers haven't tried it before. They think that students are going to come up with all kinds of wild ideas. My experience is that doesn't really happen. And the other thing is . . . it's a very common adult thing in school that we say we want the students to drive the change, but then we provide them with all the ideas.

Right here, here are the things that you can look to change instead of letting them really generate those ideas. Even in my former district, that's the area where our folks had the most difficulty—letting go and letting the kids actually come up with those ideas themselves rather than help, having us guide them to the ideas we want them to attack.

WHAT IS *NOT* TSV

When we talk with educators, almost all affirm the value of student voice. But when we push them to provide examples, they generally identify opportunities for input, such as student surveys, or forms to "hear their perspective," or opportunities for choice in things like course schedules or activities. They might point out structures for student leadership such as student councils, where students have some level of decision-making—for example, planning dances or fundraisers. While these are important, we want to emphasize that they *do not* count as Transformative Student Voice. TSV is not trivial; it is more than feedback or options. It engages *all* students, not just those in leadership roles. It is not directed by adults nor focused on topics that adults determine. It is not engaging young people as supporters of adult agendas.

HOW DO WE KNOW TSV WORKS?

Over the past fifteen years, our team has been engaged in research-practice partnerships with rural, suburban, and urban school districts across the nation. These partnerships focus on issues of school and community change, locating the voices of students as key participants in systems change approaches. We have used both quantitative and qualitative approaches to understanding how TSV processes unfold and determining the impact for students. These include classroom observations; interviews and focus groups; documentation of YPAR projects; assessments of the quality of youth policy proposals and presentations; and survey assessments of both youth and educators that measure critical reflection, political efficacy, engagement in action, leadership, ethnic identity development, sense of belonging in classrooms, and perceived relevance of school. Doing this has allowed us to develop a full curriculum for educators who wish to implement CCI and TSV, an assessment tool (both formative and summative) to measure the quality of youth policy arguments, and a range of trainings for educators to utilize both—and we are working on a project to develop an advanced set of research tools to add to our curricular resources.

We have focused on documenting young people's stories and cases of school and district change over hundreds of groups and sites over multiple years. This has allowed us to have confidence that the work is impactful in a range of settings and with a very wide range of adults and young people, and to uncover the tensions and challenges that come with engaging in work that challenges the status quo. Our quantitative approaches have been focused on student self-reported outcomes, as indicated in measures of sociopolitical development and leadership:

- TSV participants demonstrate a greater level of critical reflection and sociopolitical efficacy, and they engage in more sociopolitical action than their non-TSV peers. In addition, there is a positive relationship between years of participation in TSV and participation in sociopolitical action.[40]
- Participation in the Critical Civic Inquiry (CCI) curriculum (the curriculum that supports implementing TSV in classrooms) is a protective factor in youth ethnic identity and academic engagement.[41]

In addition to the student outcomes, our interpretive case studies include promising evidence that TSV can contribute to learning and change at multiple levels for students, for teachers, and for schools overall. Students who participated in the CCI classroom project showed increases in academic engagement, perceived relevance of school, and collaborative skills, along with developing an identity as a member of a larger community committed to social justice.[42] Teachers participating in CCI improved their capacity to share power, facilitate participatory action research, and take on leadership in their schools.[43] While changes in schools are rarer, we have documented examples where sustained systems for student participation led to more socially just and developmentally responsive school cultures.[44] In addition to documenting evidence of learning and change among students, teachers, and schools, we have focused on making visible the challenges, contradictions, and tensions in equity-centered student-driven school reform. This work is less outcome-focused and more about generating insights about complexities in the change process. In one case, for example, we complicate the literature on scaling educational innovations by showing the limits of existing frameworks and the importance of community organizing as a strategy for scaling innovation.[45] Other papers have taken up the intersections of issues of power and privilege with regard to student voice—and the challenges that teachers and school leaders experience when adapting to a more egalitarian partnership paradigm.[46]

VERTICAL INTEGRATION OF TSV

Much of the work and research on student voice has occurred at the classroom level (which we discuss in detail in our companion volume, *Transformative Student Voice for Teachers: A Guide to Classroom Action*), but in this book, we want to

FIGURE 1.2   **Examples of horizontal and vertical scaling**

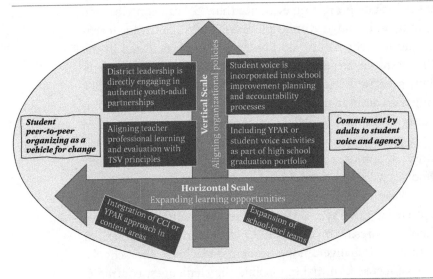

challenge you, as a leader, to consider the goal of systems change—to integrate changes across the system by evolving mindsets.[47] With that in mind, we've spent the past five years working with our partner districts on developing strategies to scale TSV vertically. Rather than just increasing the number of classrooms or opportunities for young people to engage in school transformation work, we want to be strategic in thinking about the system and about how to set up the system such that student voice is integral at all levels. Figure 1.2 creates a visual representation of what that looks like, and chapters 2 through 8 explore each element in greater depth, with case studies to illustrate the nuances of that element.

Often, efforts to scale school improvements or reforms involve starting a program, then expanding that program across classrooms or schools, thereby increasing the number of teachers and students who are impacted. This is an important step, as it lays a foundation for the work and spreads the innovation. The more challenging work, however, happens on the vertical axis—embedding the value of including students in school operations, centering their participation, and sharing power. On the vertical axis we challenge districts to ensure that key leadership is engaged in authentic youth-adult partnerships. At the board level, this means having student representation. At the superintendent level, it means having students in regular conversation with the superintendent and cabinet about the issues that concern them and the policies that impact them. Across departments, it means engaging students in meaningful ways on curriculum teams, in interview processes, and in evaluation work. This could look like:

- including students in educator hiring, professional learning, and evaluation—and ensuring that the evaluation process evaluates the degree to which teachers share power and voice with young people;
- incorporating young people in school improvement and planning processes; and
- centering TSV in the curriculum development process and graduation requirements.

In larger districts, this might mean creating a student voice office with staff, while in midsize districts it might mean hiring a coordinator for student voice. In smaller districts, the responsibility is likely to be assigned to building leadership.

TSV CHALLENGES

Although it is rarely articulated as such, the most basic premise upon which different approaches to educational policy and practice rest is trust—whether or not adults trust young people to be good (or not), to have and use relevant knowledge (or not), and to be responsible (or not). The educational institutions and practices that have prevailed in the United States, both historically and currently, reflect a basic lack of trust in students and have evolved to keep students under control and in their place as the largely passive recipients of what others determine is education.[48]

While there are some pragmatic challenges to engaging in TSV (such as resources, money, time, skill building for adults) and structural challenges (student schedules, teacher schedules, transportation, coordinating meeting times), the greater challenges are the result of fear and lack of trust. Sometimes this is internally directed: educators may be afraid of losing control, of not being seen as the expert, of not knowing the answers. Sometimes it's externally directed, such as a fear that students will not take the work seriously, or that if they do, they may fail in their initiatives and give up.

EDWARD O'NEIL, DISTRICT LEADER, USD

 I'm always going to advocate for authentic student voice, which can be scary to a lot of people because if you allow students or just the community as a whole to articulate what it is that they need and what they want and how it is delivered, it might not align with current plans or thinking that you have. And so it is not—it doesn't sit well, or there's an uneasy tension when there's already an agenda set forth. And so true and authentic student voice is one where you can't plan the outcome before the process, and that's really, really hard for some people to get.

From a pragmatic perspective, barriers in the classroom can include discomfort with unfamiliar pedagogy, misalignment with assessments, inadequate supports for professional learning, teacher identity as "expert," and the banking model of teaching, in which teachers impart information to students, who receive it without question.

At the school level, barriers include the amount of time it takes to change policy and practice while students are moving on, misalignment with school improvement initiatives, and a lack of time and space to do the work.

At the district level, barriers include the challenge of rhetoric versus reality, especially tired ideas about who gets to be part of student voice, issues of adultism, and deficit thinking.

WHAT'S NEXT

Ready to get started? In the next chapter, we'll help you plan for getting started by sharing strategies to determine the *how* that works for your district or school, including where to start, how to set the stage, how to identify the right team members (teacher-leaders, administrators, and students) to get started, how to craft the best structures, and what resources you will need. We'll talk about dispositions, mindsets, and skill development, and get specific about the challenges and barriers, with advice on how to anticipate and address them. We'll share lessons learned. The following five chapters will each showcase a specific place to focus on: curriculum, school improvement planning, district departments and initiatives, afterschool clubs or summer sessions, and engaging with community organizations. Each of these chapters will share specific stories, describe the processes and practices, outcomes, and lessons learned. Finally, we'll bring it all together by including information on how to build partnerships to support and sustain the work, generate support, build educator capacity, and assess the impact of the work.

TWO

Getting Ready

IMAGINE WITH US A SCHOOL SYSTEM in which every student, beginning in elementary school, has experienced the key elements of TSV (see chapter 3), and by the end of middle school has completed the Critical Civic Inquiry curriculum (see chapter 5). At all levels, students are included as part of school-level teams with student representation on curriculum teams, on climate teams, and on hiring committees. Student voice is central to the work of the school and district, and students take ownership of the process, policies, and personnel that make up the school experience. This would be a school system that has successfully implemented Transformative Student Voice.

Is it possible? We think so, but it requires intentional commitment to changing the system. In our largest and longest partnership (see chapter 4) we've moved from a few classrooms in a few schools to a district-level office supporting coaches and teachers in most of the district-run high schools. We've worked with that district to integrate student voice into teacher professional learning and evaluation, high school graduation requirements, and school improvement planning teams.

SETTING THE STAGE

A systems-wide approach to TSV requires leaders to consider and plan for all of the ways that TSV must be incorporated into the work of schools and districts, so we start with a framework for both vertical and horizontal integration (refer back to figure 1.2 in chapter 1). A horizontal model of integration is about the number of classrooms across multiple schools that are supporting TSV, and about the infrastructure needed at the district office level to support those sites. This is critically important if all students are to be prepared and ready to participate in TSV work. Vertical integration is about ensuring that student voice is part of every aspect of district and school decision-making; this is complicated work that requires changing mindsets and schedules and training adults in how to both value and make room for authentic student participation and voice (see figure 1.2).

If you've made it this far, we assume you are ready to imagine and plan for that possibility. You'll want a system for taking notes in this chapter as we guide you through thinking about all the places in the organizational structure where student voice should be central and included—so find a notebook or create a google folder. We will also share how to revise policy and practice to ensure that students are centered in educator hiring and evaluation, curriculum and pedagogical practices, teacher professional development and evaluation, school improvement and planning processes, and policymaking spaces. We'll guide you through strategies to help determine the *how* that works for your district or school, including where to start, how to identify the right team members (teacher-leaders, administrators, and students), how to craft the best structures, and how to secure resources.

We'll discuss the necessary dispositions, the mindset shifts that must happen, the skills that need to be developed (for adults and youth), and the challenges to anticipate when committing to what is both a process and a goal. We identify current schooling structures that are likely to be barriers to full implementation and discuss how to navigate those hurdles.

We will further highlight our lessons learned in the form of missteps to avoid, and we will support you in connecting this work to learning standards, school improvement processes, and other district-specific initiatives. By the end of the chapter, you will have a plan for building a team, getting stakeholder buy-in, and communicating the strategy to the larger community. The subsequent chapters each showcase a specific part of the education system in which we have incorporated TSV.

Horizontal and Vertical Integration

Our framework for both vertical and horizontal integration is shown in figure 1.2 in chapter 1. As noted, the horizontal model is about opportunities for students to learn the CCI/TSV curriculum, ensuring that every student has an opportunity to participate—so this is about the number of classrooms, across the number of schools, supporting TSV, and about providing the training and support that teachers need. We mean to ensure that young people are prepared to engage in TSV work by developing their skills to do so in the classroom, starting in the early grades and advancing as they grow, and by ensuring that *all* students experience our CCI curriculum, develop a critical consciousness, and conduct a YPAR project. At the same time, adult educators must be prepared to share power and work in partnership with students. Horizontal integration is perhaps the more straightforward part of the process, and we discuss it in greater detail in chapter 3.

DR. SOFIA GIANELLI, SUPERINTENDENT, DEERFIELD REGIONAL SCHOOL DISTRICT

Student voice absolutely was a big change and a positive one here. Not that we certainly weren't listening to kids, but not in that formal, structured kind of way. Students really felt heard when we follow these processes, and follow through on what they said. They started with this. And then here's how they solve their problem. It became a formalized process, and they really started to feel heard.

Vertical integration is about ensuring that student voice is part of every aspect of district decision-making, and it is complicated work that requires changing mindsets and schedules, as well as training adults to value and make room for authentic student participation and voice. In this next section, we want to focus more on the vertical axis: integrating TSV at all levels of the district and school, in all departments, truly sharing power and voice. In table 2.1, we lay out the key areas of operation within a school district, provide some examples of the *how*, and share some outcomes of including student voice in these areas.

TABLE 2.1   **Vertical integration table**

DEPARTMENT	ACTIVITIES	EXAMPLES	OUTCOMES
Human Resources	Recruiting, interviewing, supporting, evaluating	Students at Community Action Charter School are part of interview committees, crafting interview questions, interviewing potential candidates, and providing feedback. At Union City School District, middle and high school students participate in "plus delta" evaluations of learning units, which contribute to teacher evaluation and curriculum planning.	Schools experience improvement in retention of teacher hires because there is greater alignment with the student population. Instructional coaches provide better coaching and support to classroom teachers.

continued

TABLE 2.1   **Vertical integration table** *(continued)*

DEPARTMENT	ACTIVITIES	EXAMPLES	OUTCOMES
		In Urban School District (USD), student voice is part of teacher evaluation, which includes data from a student perception survey, weighted at 14 percent of the total score.	
Curriculum, Pedagogy, Assessment	Curriculum development, resource selection, pedagogical feedback, assessment	Students at Urban Arts Academy worked with district curriculum designers to plan a comprehensive health unit, urging the district to include certain content around consent and to use more engaging pedagogies. USD students advocating for a Student Bill of Rights publicly urged the district to offer real-world skills, such as financial literacy, as well as more culturally relevant content. District curriculum specialists then collaborated with students to improve the civics curriculum.	Schools or districts offer curriculum that is more grounded in students' lived experience and fosters deeper engagement and learning.
Professional Development	Training for teachers and staff	Urban Arts Academy students have engaged in a yearslong project of designing and implementing professional development units for their teachers around cultural competence; the district has lauded their efforts and used them as an exemplar for other schools to also offer youth-led professional development. In Deerfield Regional School District, students worked with the professional development team to create vignettes of biased comments they experienced, and led a program for teachers in which they provided the vignette, asked teachers to discuss what they thought happened (or what should have happened), then shared what actually happened and what they wished had happened.	Teachers learn more about how students perceive their experiences, and they have real-world examples of the challenges and perspectives of the students they care about. Students are empowered to share their own experiences and to think about what teachers need to know.

continued

TABLE 2.1   **Vertical integration table** *(continued)*

DEPARTMENT	ACTIVITIES	EXAMPLES	OUTCOMES
Business Office	Budgets, school expenditures, strategic planning, scheduling, school improvement planning	At the New Outlook Academy, students lobbied the district to allocate more resources to schools that serve students who have been expelled or are involved with the justice system. The youth have met with district officials, but little has changed yet. The students and their teacher continue to surface this issue with district officials. In the Rural Schools Climate Project, students from four small, rural districts on the eastern seaboard served on climate teams and helped to develop the values statements guiding climate work. They made recommendations for sensory pathways, wellness rooms, and possible bathroom policies, and they helped with the design, implementation, and evaluation of those suggestions.	Districts and schools that engage stakeholders, including students, in decision-making and planning experience higher levels of engagement, participation, and buy-in.
Culture, Climate, Discipline		Students from the Creative Arts Academy noticed that the school dress code disproportionately targeted female-identifying students. They worked with school leaders to challenge gender biases within the dress code and in how it was being enforced by teachers. Young women at the Justice School noticed that a lack of access to feminine hygiene products provided barriers to learning; they worked with Planned Parenthood to install menstruation stations with free products in school bathrooms.	Schools become more inclusive spaces, discipline incidents are reduced, and culture is improved.
Scheduling, Logistics		Students at Plains View High School noticed that poor transportation options in the district and community resulted in large numbers of tardies. While the district could provide little support because of a driver shortage, the city transit system promised a new bus line to the school within two years.	

continued

TABLE 2.1   **Vertical integration table** *(continued)*

DEPARTMENT	ACTIVITIES	EXAMPLES	OUTCOMES
		After learning about TSV at a workshop, school board members paused a planned renovation of the school playground to invite student feedback. They scheduled a series of meetings with youth and solicited feedback on what they wanted on the schoolyard.	Schools and districts are made aware of barriers that may not be obvious, and they can improve accessibility and engagement.
Data Evaluation		The principal at Creative Arts Academy used data generated by the YPAR team as part of his reasoning as to why structural changes needed to be made. He also spoke to the impact the YPAR team has had on the school decision-making committee by presenting the knowledge they have generated.	Schools and districts have access to more data sources to inform their decisions, thus better meeting the needs of students.
		An Oceanside School Board member spoke to how the YPAR program in their district facilitated a data-informed mindset for adults. Youth-generated data helped provide a basis for how decisions were made and how to assess for impact later on.	
		Students at Mountain View High School examined their school perception survey (with nearly 1,500 responses) and identified themes and patterns. They proposed a tiered system of reform to address mental health issues, including the stigma around seeking support.	

GETTING STARTED

Prepare the Ground

When we talk about getting started in this section, we are still focused on helping you, as the leader, figure out your strategy. This is still "prework," if you will. You'll get started forming a team later. You may be wondering why, given our principle of sharing power and voice with students, we are focused on helping you, the leader, do the preliminary planning without involving the young people? Whether you are starting student voice work because it's the right thing to do or in response to external pressures, how you structure and communicate the initiative is important to its long-term success. With that in mind, grab your notes and respond to the following questions:

Where are you starting? Are you considering TSV because you believe it is the right thing to do? Or do you have students protesting and demanding a voice? Do you have teachers or families or board members who want to see more student voice? Whichever reason, your best starting point is to figure out how to communicate your *why*, map your system, and convene a team of allies.

What is your **why?** You picked up this book for a reason. And maybe, having read this far, we've given you more reasons to commit to TSV. But can you communicate that to students, families, community, faculty, staff, colleagues, and board members? Create an elevator pitch that explains the what and why in a short and compelling way. Maybe connect it to the mission and vision for your district or school, or to your strategic plan goals, or to your core values. Maybe connect it to data; we know that increasing student voice impacts learning and engagement. Appendix A includes a one-page evidence sheet about the benefits of student voice if you need a place to start.

Map the system

When we think about how to integrate TSV in a system in ways that will ensure that it becomes not just *another thing to do*, but a part of *how we do what we do*, we must consider how to integrate on both the horizontal and vertical axes. This means that we need to build the skills of students and teachers to do TSV in the classroom (horizontally) and make changes to policy and practice at the system level (vertically) to create the space—and accountability—for the change to occur. So, get out those notes and create your first graphic: an organization chart of your district or school. Who are the key players? What are they responsible for? What are the key initiatives? Where is there room for including TSV in each? Refer to this image to assist with your thinking. Don't get overwhelmed—at this point, you are identifying places where student voice could and should be, but you'll likely start by picking just a few areas to build from.

Make a list of allies

Who are the teachers who already advocate for student voice? Who are the students who step up to challenge the status quo? (By this we mean not just your junior leaders and volunteers—we want all the students who call out the problems they see.) Who are the family or community members who show up and engage with young people? Now expand your list. Who are the people, especially those in positions of power, who might resist or have a hard time imagining how to include students? How will your HR director, business manager, and department heads respond? How do you think your board will react? Are there community organizations that you'll need to partner with? List the arguments you think they might have. Consider your response to each and revisit your *why*. You might use the categories in table 2.1 to complete this section.

Communicate

Get strategic about your communication plan ahead of everything else. Centering student voice and inviting students to participate in decision-making are major paradigm shifts for most adults and educators. You'll need to have buy-in from your board, families, students, and educators, and a strategy for dealing with naysayers. You'll need to understand what people need and how to message TSV in a way that they see it as meeting a need. Developing a plan for communication may mean developing a formal presentation for the board, but it may mean just having some conversations over coffee with certain strategic people to get them interested first. What do you want to say to the people you'll invite to be on the team? Build that elevator pitch, which conveys what it is that you are trying to do, in a few short and powerful sentences. Make sure the connections to your larger district or school mission, vision, and strategic goals are clear.

- It's partly the messaging and knowing what people need.
- It's partly brokering, networking, and inviting the right people to the table.
- It's partly about partnering with other organizations and advocacy groups—know who is out there doing what, and how that fits into your plan.

Build Your Team

Now that you have mapped the district and people, it's time to identify the right people to get you started. Don't make the team so big that you can't get anything done, but make sure it includes a range of perspectives. A few students, educators, administrators, and community members can be a good starting point—and pay attention to demographics. As you consider the makeup of your team, know that representation matters—students want to see adults "like them" in these conversations. There are differences in how these conversations unfold when led by white teachers or leaders or by teachers or leaders of color. We have also seen how all educators and leaders hold varied beliefs about the role of young people and the challenges of schooling, irrespective of demographic, so *all* adults who engage with TSV work must be willing to engage in the development of their own critical consciousness. Once you've selected some possible candidates, share chapter 1 with them and invite them to a conversation. You'll want to consider the following dispositions or mindsets as you interview people for your team. Appendix B has some helpful questions and an interview protocol you can use.

- How do they view the role of adults and students? Do they need to be the one who *knows* and has the right answers, or are they open to new ideas and to student perspectives? Do they view students as needing to listen and learn? To do what adults say the first time, every time?
- How do they view the idea of respect? Is it an issue of authority, or is respect due to everyone based on their individual humanity?
- Are they afraid of retaliation, mistakes, failure, or critique?

DEREK WHITE, TEACHER, USD

As I tell my students, "My goal here is to help you stay organized and open these meetings. I'll send a recap email and I could be the note taker, but this is your process." And so student leaders like Tanisha, Jamar, Camika, Nick, and Julia kind of stepped up right away, and just led it, so I didn't have really much to do with the creating, really anything to do [with] the creation of [the] bill, other than some light editing. Occasionally I'd throw out some ideas, but you know they really completely led that, that entire process, and I was just, you know, keeping them hyped up, creating breakout rooms, keeping them motivated, that was really all I did.

Plan your first team meetings

As you plan your first few team meetings, think about the following ideas, and make sure you have time to do the team building, foundation building, and setting norms that will ensure a strong team. (Again, see appendix B if you need a list of helpful interview questions.)

- How will you build a sense of team? What will you do to help the team members get to know each other? What are the group norms that will guide your interactions? How will you make decisions?
- You did a lot of preplanning work—how will you share or modify your vision and communications? Will you have the team do some of the same activities you did to get ready in the earlier part of this chapter? Or will you share your ideas for the team to provide feedback and revisions?
- You'll want to discuss the horizontal and vertical aspects of implementing TSV and begin planning for both phases of implementation—do you start in one building or all of them? As an afterschool program or club, or as part of the curriculum? Will you have the team read this book, so they understand the range of options, or will you summarize? Are there choices that you will take off the table? Why?
- How will you identify and train the educators who are going to lead the work? What is your strategy for doing some of the training work with this team?
- How are you going to develop an action plan with your team? What is the long-term goal? What are the first steps?

Decision-Making Protocols

There are multiple ways to make decisions, and it's critical that your team has conversations about which approach you will use.

Often in the day-to-day work of districts and schools, the approach is that the leader (superintendent, director, principal, or administrator) will decide—they may collect input from others, but ultimately they'll choose and then inform everyone else. Or they may delegate the decision-making to someone.

The formal structure of school governance, such as a school board, likely uses a majority rule approach, where members vote, and the most votes wins. This is a familiar approach, but it creates a winner-loser dynamic and often reinforces the status quo.

While these approaches might feel comfortable, they don't really address one of the core values of student voice—the idea of *sharing power and voice*. What does? A consensus-based model of decision-making.

Consensus-based models are challenging, as they often require more time. They don't necessarily mean unanimous support, but they do mean that everyone has an opportunity to be heard, all the perspectives are considered, and everyone on the team can at least live with the decision to be made.

Our favorite resource for learning about and using a consensus-based model is available on the Seeds for Change website.[1] It includes processes and protocols that help with facilitating and skill building.

Developing Norms and Agreements

You are probably familiar with the practice of setting norms for group meetings. We'd like to advocate for a shift to the language of *agreements* that are collaboratively developed and that all participants can agree to. It is important in this process to remind adults to be open to the language used by youth and to the critical need to define terms.

You should start with a blank slate: ask everyone in the group to write on sticky notes the things that they need to have to feel safety, respect, and trust, and to be able to participate fully. Look for patterns and themes, talk about how each item looks and feels, go over what each word means. One of my favorite youth-generated agreements is "Don't yuck my yum," which is an awesome way of conveying the importance of not being judgmental or critical of things that other people like or value.

Once you've created a list of possible agreements, it might be helpful to review some core ideas to make sure you have covered all the important topics. The organization Heart-Mind Online has a list of eleven common elements that promote a safe group environment—making sure you've covered all of those will help ensure that you have solid agreements.[2] Another favorite resource is the REDI agreements, created by the Equity Lab, which are designed to explicitly deal with issues of race and equity.[3]

Make sure you set aside sufficient time for a first brainstorming session as well as for a few follow-up sessions to refine and adjust the agreements. It's also important to have a plan to revisit the agreements. Keep them posted at the beginning of each meeting, and maybe use them as an icebreaker to get started— I like to ask people to share examples of one that they've seen done well since we last met. Continue to discuss how they are working at points throughout the cycle of team meetings, and discuss them whenever conflict arises. It's also helpful to have a plan for how you will call out or call in violations of the agreements—something as simple as "Ouch" can be a signal that an agreement has been violated.

Create Your Structures

Structurally, the size and organization of your district matters. Our largest partner district (USD, with nearly ninety thousand students) has an office of student voice, which supports coaches and teachers, coordinates curriculum, and works across initiatives.[4] In smaller districts, responsibility often falls under the mandate of an assistant superintendent or director. In schools, it's too often tasked to "that one great teacher," but it needs to be an expectation for all adults.

So the first structural change? Make centering students in decision-making a core value of the district, central to your strategic plan. Make it part of all leadership evaluations. Make it a question that is asked of every initiative or decision (*How are students included in this?*) Include funding for student voice work and training in your budgets and also in your grant applications.

Then allocate training, time, and funding to ensure that students are centered. Make it the very specific responsibility of someone, and make sure that time and resources are allocated to support teachers, buildings, and departments as they revise their policies and practices to center student voice. If you are in a large district, maybe you can hire a coordinator specific to student voice. If you are in a smaller district, maybe it becomes the responsibility of your climate leaders. At the building level, assign a teacher, and give them time, support, and a stipend.

MERCEDES SOSA, DIRECTOR OF YOUTH LEADERSHIP, USD

So I think that's always one thing that comes up for us, is like there's always a sense of feeling of, there needs to be more preparedness before involving student voice, and us being like "Well, if by more preparedness you mean more decision-making to then have young people at the end as tokens, that's not what we're trying to do." So that's always like a hard conversation. So that ended up having to be paused and then you know with the commitment of Colin and I meeting at the beginning of next year to really figure out like, how do we start embedding training for adults? So that they check their bias and their adultism, and then to then be able to then introduce young people to the work and have them be decision-makers and whatever their schools are doing.

Barriers and Missteps

The following five issues stand out when we look back at the barriers that our districts have had to overcome.

Finding Time

How do you set aside time to train and support the coaches and teachers? How do you find time in the day to build student voice work into the curriculum? How do you make sure that there is time on each meeting agenda to ask the question, "Where is the student voice in this decision, policy, or practice?"

Mindset shifts and skill development

How do you ensure that adults will actually listen to the proposals and ideas of young people? What is the forum for that? How do you grapple with adultist or paternalistic mindsets and the assumption that adults know the answers and students don't?

Questions to ask yourself to identify potential issues with adultism:

- "Would I treat an adult this way?"
- "Would I talk to an adult in this tone of voice?"
- "Would I grab this out of an adult's hand?"
- "Would I make this decision for an adult?"
- "Would I have this expectation of an adult?"
- "Would I limit an adult's behavior this way?"
- "Would I listen to an adult friend's problem in this same way?"[5]

Structural segregation

Schools are structured around age segregation, and the job routines of many adults who work in school districts keep them segregated from the youth, who are in different buildings and in scheduled classes or activities (the larger the district, the bigger problem this becomes). Meeting schedules rarely account for or accommodate student schedules or transportation needs. This combination of time, schedules, and spatial geography is a barrier to be addressed.

Lack of resources

We've said it many times throughout this chapter, but time, money, and training are the big three resources. You need to support teachers with time to plan, implement, and attend training. And you must figure out how to give students the time and access to transportation that they need in order to fully participate.

Lack of stamina

Structural changes don't happen overnight, and we've seen too many times how pressing issues take over and push out visionary ideas. Committing to making your school or district a space that centers student voice, supports student voice, and integrates student voice in all elements of the district is a long-term commitment, not a onetime activity with immediate results.

EDWARD O'NEIL, COLLEGE AND CAREER DEPARTMENT HEAD, USD

 O'Neil remains steady in his commitment to student voice, but also to acknowledging the complexity of making it a consistent part of the work of the district.

> Part of my role is making sure as leaders and people who are working with students that we do empower them to lead, we do make sure that they understand their brilliance, and that sometimes ... we get out of the way.

He sees his role as supporting the leaders who report to him, asking them questions to ensure they are including students, and keeping connected to students by "popping in" to classrooms and engaging with them.

> with my team, when we discuss things or are planning things, I always want to know how does it involve and—number one— how does it benefit students? How do we know that? And

how it involves students. Do we know it will benefit students? Are we putting them first by what we think, or have we actually engaged with students to understand that and their perspective? I try to lead in a way that encourages student voice.

He's clear about the complexity of getting beyond simply allowing student input, but also sees the value of that input—and he appreciates the challenge of getting adults to fully commit to sharing power with students rather than using them to support adult goals. He names this as a required paradigm shift.

> I'm always going to advocate for authentic student voice, which can be scary to a lot of people, because if you allow students or just the community as a whole to articulate what it is that they need and what they want and how it is delivered, it might not align with current plans or thinking that you have.

CONCLUSION

Our first chapter laid out the challenges of changing systems, along with the history and definition of Transformative Student Voice, and this chapter was designed to assist you with the practical matters of getting ready: structuring your team to plan and implement the initiatives that will support the transition to TSV in your school or district. In the next five chapters, we share examples of the range of ways in which TSV has been implemented in the schools and districts we work with—from embedding it into the curriculum, to hosting afterschool clubs or summer sessions, to including young people in school and district teams, to partnering with external organizations. Each chapter has examples and stories, tools, and resources. We invite you to read these, and discuss them as a team, in order to guide your planning for how you will integrate TSV both horizontally and vertically in your schools and districts.

THREE

School Improvement Planning and School Reform

WHILE WE HAVE MADE THE ARGUMENT in the opening chapters for including student voice in all aspects of schooling, in this chapter we argue for the importance of centering students and their voices in the processes related to school improvement, strategic planning, and transformation and reform. It is the arena with the most long-term cost and consequence, but, at best, usually only includes student input through surveys. We'll take you through three levels of student voice, as shown in figure 3.1.

THREE LEVELS OF STUDENT VOICE

If you are committed to Transformative Student Voice, you must work to center students at all three levels. In the sections below, we'll provide definitions and examples of each.[1]

The base level is *advisor.* This level is about ensuring student input, and all students in the school should have opportunities to contribute at this level. It could include having a suggestion box—physical or electronic—for raising concerns, or

FIGURE 3.1 **Three levels of student voice**

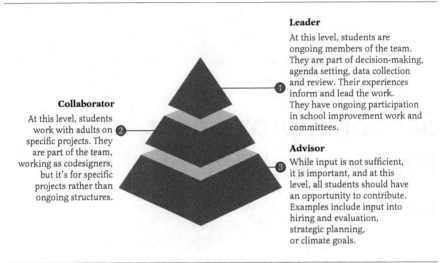

Leader

At this level, students are ongoing members of the team. They are part of decision-making, agenda setting, data collection and review. Their experiences inform and lead the work. They have ongoing participation in school improvement work and committees.

Collaborator

At this level, students work with adults on specific projects. They are part of the team, working as codesigners, but it's for specific projects rather than ongoing structures.

Advisor

While input is not sufficient, it is important, and at this level, all students should have an opportunity to contribute. Examples include input into hiring and evaluation, strategic planning, or climate goals.

surveys about school climate or other issues under consideration. It might include conversations, such as when a superintendent or principal convenes a group of students to ask their opinions on an idea or concern. The distinguishing characteristic of this level is that students are given the opportunity to provide input, but the adults choose what to do with that input—it is advisory, in that it informs adult decision-making. It is important to include students at this level, and equally important to close the loop of communication. When you ask students for input, make sure to share the survey results and the decisions made as a result of their input. If you can't do what students suggest, provide a reason why and an alternative plan.

In Union City School District, leadership sought regular feedback from students about proposed changes to schedules, course offerings, school climate, and other topics, using surveys to collect that input. However, students thought that they didn't pay attention to their responses. The lesson? Always share the results and how they informed your decisions. Close that feedback loop.

The next level is *collaborator*. At this level, adults and youth are working together on a specific issue or topic. They may be coplanning a professional development exercise; they may be collaborating on a curriculum; they may be designing a climate survey or a community space. The student's role is more than input or advice, as there is a tangible product or outcome, but it's a onetime project rather than an ongoing process. The group might meet a few times or over the course of a longer span of time, but it has a clear task to accomplish, and it will disband when the goal is complete. This level is about an intentional invitation for students to assist in devising solutions to a specific issue.

The final level is *leader*. This does not mean that students are in charge, rather it indicates a level of engagement on standing committees that make decisions about policy and governance. It's about coleading with adults on school improvement committees, strategic planning committees, curriculum committees, or data review committees. It might include student representatives on the board of education. The commitment is to sharing leadership (power and voice) with students in the ongoing, sustained work of the school or district.

We'll start with an example of an equity council in Noble Township—a midsize district on the East Coast—that incorporated students as regular members of that team (leader level), and we'll talk about how they set themselves up for success, the challenges they had to grapple with, and the logistics that made it work. We'll then unpack an example from South Country School District, which engaged with students to solve a more bounded problem (collaborator level) and provides an example of an ongoing student advisory structure (advisor level). Finally, we'll share how a research-practice partnership between four small school districts on the East Coast and their local university (the Rural Schools Climate Project) engaged in a four-year school climate transformation grant, and we will explore their challenges, opportunities, and missteps as they worked to center the voices of students in the transformation process.

Students as (Co)leaders

Noble Township is a district with a high-achieving school system serving over seven thousand students, with a population that is 74 percent white, 9 percent Black, 9 percent Latine, 4 percent Asian, and only 10 percent are eligible for free or reduced-price lunch. The township voters are evenly split between Democrats and Republicans, and the median household income is $106,000. A student-led protest over racist text messages in 2018 created a media flurry and propelled the issues of racial equity in the district to the school board's attention, resulting in the development of an equity committee made up of families, educators, and students and a contract with national equity consultants. This account picks up after COVID-19 restrictions had ended, in 2022.

Three students regularly attended the equity committee, which had fifteen to twenty members, including a mix of families, teachers, and administration officials, with political affiliations ranging from Christian conservative to liberal/progressive. Tamara, a Black female student, joined as a junior at the invitation of Ms. Johnson, a white female teacher who was on the committee. Angie, a white female, joined at the end of the second year; she identifies as part of the LGBTQIA+ community and was also recommended by Ms. Johnson. Ariel, a biracial Asian/white female, started attending from the beginning, along with her mother, who was also on the committee. The students participated in all committee activities, starting with an eight-part training on the foundations of DEI work, progressing through a series of data dives looking at district data, and culminating in the development of an equity plan and formal bylaws for the committee. The students often raised issues or counternarratives that showed a different point of view from the adults. For example, when we were developing the school safety goal of the equity plan, the adults on the committee were in agreement that adding more school resource officers (SROs) would be an important part of the plan, but Tamara spoke up to say that all students did not feel positive about that idea—in fact, they felt unsafe in the presence of the SROs. Many of the adult council members were surprised and taken aback by that statement. But Ms. Johnson helped create space for Tamara to advocate for her position, resulting in the group agreeing to have the plan address the students' sense of bodily safety in the presence of the SROs, rather than just advocating for more SROs. This was a challenging moment for the committee—the principal listened to Tamara's perspective (which was supported by Ariel), but struggled to understand how students could feel unsafe in the presence of SROs.

Many times during the equity council meetings (that are still happening monthly as of this writing), student perspectives extended and expanded the perception that adults—both families and educators—had about an issue. These have included conversations about curriculum (*Should* The Bluest Eye *be a required reading?*) and about policy and practices (*Should gender neutral bathrooms be available in every wing? Should period products be available in all restrooms, even those designated "male"?*). The power dynamics among administrators, teachers, families, and students could shut out the voices of students, but the structure of the council, and the time we spent on the foundational training, created a set of skills in both adults and students to mediate those default reactions.

The outcome of engaging students in the equity council? Strategic goals and policy changes that represent the actual perspective and experiences of students, and an expanded

FIGURE 3.2 **Being an ally**

Topic and Title	Learning Outcomes
Exploring Identity	- understand the idea of critical consciousness - explore the things that influence the development of identity - develop an understanding of the "Big 8" social identities
Understanding Culture	- examine the elements that constitute "culture" - understand cultural norms and values - explore your own cultural experiences
Power and Privilege	- analyze the danger of a single story - explore why difference matters within an intercultural mindset - practice understanding other perspectives
Difference: Perspective Taking	- explore how power and privilege operate - examine the link between individual experiences and the influence of systems - learn how to talk about privilege with others
Implicit Bias	- discover how bias works - understand how implicit biases develop - learn how to identify your own biases
Microaggressions	- examine how microaggressions occur - understand the harm of microaggressions - outline ways to address microaggressions
The Power of Words	- evaluate the power of words - understand how language can exclude people - develop inclusive language
Being an Ally, Accomplice, or Advocate	- learn when to be an ally, accomplice, or advocate

understanding, on the part of adults, about those student experiences. Strategies to make it work? The committee meets from 6 to 8 p.m. so that families and students can attend. The foundational training in allyship and DEI work (see figure 3.2) and use of the REDI agreements (see figure 3.3) helped all parties get to the point of consensus.

Both adults and students developed the skills needed to listen, to speak their truths, to examine other perspectives,

FIGURE 3.3   **REDI agreements**

REDI Agreements
• Stay engaged.
• Speak your truth.
• Experience discomfort.
• Give and get grace.
• Observe the 24–48 hours rule.
• Expect/accept lack of closure.
• Notice patterns of participation.
• Respect confidentiality.
• Recognize intent vs. impact.
• Consider power dynamics.
• Recognize the danger of a single story.

Source: Glenn E. Singleton and Curtis Linton, *Courageous Conversations About Race: A Field Guide for Achieving Equity in Schools*, 1st ed. (Thousand Oaks, CA: Corwin Press, 2005).

and to engage as allies. The looming challenge? All three students are set to graduate this coming year—so a process for recruiting new participants, including students, is under discussion.

> An important tension to address when recruiting new participants: Are the students (and other members) representing themselves and their opinions, or are they to represent the broader student body? How can you accomplish this while ensuring demographic representation and elevating the perspectives of the most marginalized groups?

Students as Collaborators

At Deerfield, as part of their ongoing equity work, a teacher met with a group of students during their Wednesday extended lunch period to engage in a TSV project. High school students in the TSV group identified a problem with microaggressions among their peers, and they designed a survey for the students that asked questions about their experiences with microaggressions. They then analyzed that data and presented it to the faculty, along with a series of asks: They wanted to see the history and English language arts (ELA) curricula expanded to include more representation of diverse histories and perspectives about race, gender, and sexuality. They wanted a seat on the equity council (which did not currently include students)—a leadership level ask. And they wanted to help create professional development for teachers and character education lessons for students to address the concerns identified in the survey. They worked with members of the equity council to design a professional development workshop for teachers that included vignettes of actual experiences they had with microaggressions in the classrooms and hallways, and they invited teachers to talk about how they would respond to those scenarios. They then shared with teachers what had actually happened in each instance (which was rarely the way teachers claimed they would respond) and shared how they *wanted* teachers to respond when those things happened. While this was a onetime professional development event, the fact that they used data generated by students and partnered with them to design and deliver solutions makes this fit under the banner of project-specific collaborations.

The outcome of engaging students in the planning for the professional development? Teachers got to experience a powerful workshop that represented the actual perspective and experiences of students, and they got to hear from the students about what they needed from adults to have a safer, more inclusive school climate. The strategies that made it work? The foundational training in DEI work and the use of the REDI agreements (again, see figures 3.2 and 3.3) helped both adults and students work together to design the workshop. The lack of protected time was a challenge, but the students' and lead teacher's commitment to using their own extended lunch made it work.

In another example of collaboration, at Community Action Charter School, students were part of the hiring process for both staff and administration. In this grade 6-12 school, a commitment to shared governance was a core value, and so families, students, and staff were engaged in the hiring process. At the student level, anyone who wanted to volunteer to be on the hiring committee could. Planning meetings happened, in which job postings were reviewed and edited and interview processes and questions were designed. Typically, interviews for all positions happened on a Saturday, with candidates doing a rotation through different rooms, interviewing with panels of families, staff, and students. One year, when the principal role was open, Shelley collaborated with the student group to discuss the job description, recruiting materials, and suggestions for edits. They discussed what the students valued in a principal—the characteristics and skills they wanted that person to have. The group discussed the kinds of questions they wanted to ask, and what would help them really know who the candidate was. Students came up with great questions and a few scenarios, and then Marshawn had a brilliant idea: he asked, "What if I do something during the interview that could be seen as disrespectful or rude, and we see how they handle it?" The rest of the group loved the idea, and so when interviews were happening (in a classroom with chairs around a cluster of desks), Marshawn leaned back and put his foot on the table. Each of the three candidates reacted differently. One stared at him, and his foot, but didn't say anything. One addressed him directly, saying, "It's rude to put your feet on the table—please don't." The final candidate paused, looked around at the group, and asked if being that relaxed and comfortable was because they liked him, or if it was part of the school's cultural norms. The reaction and responses to the questions, the vignette, and the "test" informed their feedback to the school board, which would ultimately make the decision about who to hire.

Students as Advisors

In Union City Schools, all teachers were expected to include a "plus delta" process (asking students to identify what worked—the plus—and what should change—the delta) after each curricular unit for students to provide feedback on the content, the class, and the assignments. Students appreciated the opportunity to provide feedback and noted that some teachers really did use that feedback to improve their classes, while others were inconsistent.

Shelley and her team had been working with three local districts over several years to address equity issues in their school systems, and they had developed a robust student voice team at one of the districts. Then the US Department of Education released a call for proposals for school-university partnerships to implement a multitiered system of support for improving school climate, including the need for respectful interaction and skill development for citizenship as crucial elements of that work. Eight total schools (elementary and middle schools in each of four districts) participated over the course of the project, serving a total of 2,930 students. The team called the project "The Case for Student Voice as a Change Agent in Schools: A Focus on Culturally Responsive Climate, Equity, and Discipline," and they were funded $2.4 million over four years.

Necessary, but Not Sufficient

You may already have a student rep on the school board, or you may invite students to provide input on some things, some of the time. In the multiple districts we work with, the superintendent hosts regular sessions with students to hear their perspectives and get their input. This is a good thing to do, but is likely not sufficient to meet the expectations of TSV—and often does not include a diverse range of students, both demographically (race, gender, socioeconomic status) and by their level of success in schools (academic achievement, good behavior). This type of "advising" should be one of a range of ways that students participate, and not the only way.

Many readers may be familiar with the structure of the MTSS (Multitiered System of Supports), and likely with the system of PBIS/PBSIS (Positive Behavior Interventions and Supports or Positive Behavior Support in Schools), which has been a popular behavioral intervention in schools nationwide since the early 2000s. What has always been interesting is that the design of the PBIS systems *requires* that 80 percent of adults in a building are on board, and that they participate in the design—but there is no requirement for student voice and input. This was the central innovation Shelley's team wanted to implement, leveraging the power and possibility of engaging youth as cocreators of positive school climate, and promoting students' social-emotional development, engagement with school, and academic achievement.

They asked the participating schools to ensure that there was dedicated time and space for students (both in the classroom and on leadership teams) to learn together, do research, develop policy proposals, and share their work with school and district personnel. They also required that student participants were reflective of the diversity of each school community, with priority given to recruiting and retaining students who were struggling or least-served by the current system; that stakeholders were committed to leaning in to critical conversations about power and privilege, identity, and systems of oppression; and that students and teachers would participate in learning and skill development in three areas: youth-adult partnerships, educational equity, and participatory action research.

What went well? They included students in the development of the core values for their school—the whole student body engaged in the same process that adults did, identifying what a good school climate felt like, what the values were, what the expectations looked like, and how students would learn those and be supported if they struggled. Each school also created a student voice club (more on that in chapter 6), which took up specific issues related to climate for the adult climate team to consider and implement. Students at one elementary school worked with adults to design a sensory pathway. At a middle school, students advocated for and created a plan and rules to govern the creation of a wellness room.

Where did they fail? Students were not part of the ongoing work of the climate teams. Why? It's a challenge in its own right to get adults in schools to engage in climate teamwork. The team had a large grant and were paying the members for their time to participate in training and in monthly meetings, but these all happened during the school day. Leadership matters—in districts where the superintendent made this work central to their vision for the district, climate team members were more engaged, work happened outside the meeting times, and progress happened. In districts where the superintendent did not make the same visible commitment, and thus their teams were less engaged, they accomplished less. COVID-19 also hit during the first year of the grant, and that created some obvious obstacles. Principal turnover in each district shifted the focus to getting the new leaders up to speed and away from the actual work for a period of time. In sum, the team had hoped to truly create a Transformative Student Voice system in the districts, and they did achieve some level of advisory and collaborator inclusion of students—but they didn't get to the level of student leaders, which is what would have made it transformational.

MAKING IT WORK

As these examples show, including students in school improvement planning and reform can be connected to an immediate issue, a onetime challenge, or a longer-term process—all are valuable and important ways to include young people in the work of school improvement. In this section, we'll explore the context and preparation that allowed these initiatives to be successful in including students, and we'll talk about the challenges and barriers to meaningful inclusion.

Foundations

In both Noble Township and Deerfield, the adults who were part of the equity councils had a significant amount of preparation. It was not specifically focused on student voice, but instead focused on building a common language and commitment to diversity, equity, inclusion, belonging, and justice. Both groups had engaged in approximately sixteen hours of training, on topics ranging from identity development, to perspective-taking, to being an ally (see figure 3.2), and had committed to and practiced using the REDI agreements (see figure 3.3) to guide their own behavior within the group. They had some conflicts arise over the course of the eight months that they were engaged in that training, and therefore had conversations about and practice resolving those conflicts. And they knew that they were in this for the long run—that the work of the equity council was a long-term commitment to challenging and changing the status quo. So in spite of the occasional struggles that individual group members had when making space for young people, there were always group members who were ready to make space, and that helped to make sure that the group shifted and addressed the tensions. In the ongoing equity council work, an external consultant (in this case, Shelley) was at all the meetings, assisting the teams in their training and implementation. Shelley had also trained the Deerfield group but was not present during the planning with students. At both districts, several teachers (at least one of whom was on the equity council) had participated in a two-day training on implementing Transformative Student Voice, using the curriculum we discuss in chapter 5.

Getting Started

If you followed the structure and strategies in chapter 2, you have a team, and you've done some work to identify the places where students are, can, and should be included. You've identified the people who are likely to be allies and the resistance you might encounter. You've developed your communication strategies. Now it's time for your team to bring it all together and develop a five-year plan for making your school or district a TSV school or district. Make a list of all the standing committees in your district and schools, and brainstorm how you could include students on them. Make a list of all the opportunities for data collection and review. Do students participate in surveys and evaluations? When data is shared, especially climate and discipline data, are students included in the meaning-making about that data? How do your hiring processes work? Could students have a part? What about curriculum design and approval? Could they play a role? Work with your team to set three to five goals for engaging students as advisors, collaborators, and coleaders. Make the goals specific and assign responsibility for the task. For example, if you want students on the curriculum review team, assign that to the curriculum director. Set deadlines, and plan for how you will evaluate progress. Figure out what resources are needed and how you will communicate the plan to the larger school or district community. And use the rubric we provide in table 3.1 to check the quality of your plan.

TABLE 3.1 An emerging rubric for designing and evaluating student voice approaches in educational systems change efforts

	RANGE OF *ACTIVITIES IN WHICH YOUTH CAN PARTICIPATE, ROLES THEY PLAY, AND LEVELS OF PARTICIPATION OPEN TO YOUTH*	ATTENTION TO *POWER, CULTURAL CAPITAL, AND STUDENT DEMOGRAPHIC REPRESENTATION*	DEPTH AND QUALITY OF *TRAINING PROVIDED TO YOUTH AND ADULTS*	*INFRASTRUCTURE* (STAFFING, FUNDING, POLICIES, STRUCTURES, PROCESSES, RELATIONSHIP TO OTHER DEPARTMENTS AND ORGANIZATIONS, ETC.)
Basic Practice: Traditional efforts in classroom and schools	Student opinions are solicited; standard structures such as student councils and clubs exist; classroom and school practices presume that adults choose and that students comply.	Student participants represent "typical" kids and only those who are successful in school.	No training or skill building is provided.	Adult involvement in student voice work is limited to those who volunteer to lead a club or initiate it on their own. Few or no resources are provided to support such activities. No policies require student input or involvement.
Emergent Practice: More empowered students in classrooms and schools	Students have multiple opportunities to provide feedback and to engage in activities designed to improve the school, but these are limited to a traditional focus on student engagement in preset school goals. May include students in determining classroom practices, but they have a limited role in conceptualizing, designing, implementing and/or evaluating reform work.	Efforts are made to ensure participation of diverse students, e.g., those with disabilities; different genders, races, ethnicities, and languages; different levels of success in school; etc. Efforts are made to attend to the voices and perspectives of those students.	Some training is provided, but is directed at youth.	Teachers are invited to include student voices in classroom decision-making, but additional resources to support that work, or to remove barriers created by curriculum or schedules are not addressed. Training in how to do so is not provided, and successful inclusion of student voice is not part of the reward or evaluation structure for adults.

continued

TABLE 3.1 An emerging rubric for designing and evaluating student voice approaches in educational systems change efforts *(continued)*

	RANGE OF *ACTIVITIES IN WHICH YOUTH CAN PARTICIPATE, ROLES THEY PLAY, AND LEVELS OF PARTICIPATION* OPEN TO YOUTH	ATTENTION TO *POWER, CULTURAL CAPITAL, AND STUDENT DEMOGRAPHIC* REPRESENTATION	DEPTH AND QUALITY OF *TRAINING* PROVIDED TO YOUTH AND ADULTS	*INFRASTRUCTURE* (STAFFING, FUNDING, POLICIES, STRUCTURES, PROCESSES, RELATIONSHIP TO OTHER DEPARTMENTS AND ORGANIZATIONS, ETC.)
Powerful Practice: Empowered students in classrooms, schools, communities, and districts	Students are engaged in leadership roles in all decision-making groups at the school, in the district, and in the community; students participate in choosing issues to focus on, developing data collection methods, collecting data, analyzing data, making recommendations, and implementing and evaluating changes. Robust systems exist for youth to participate in ongoing ways in the conceptualization, design, implementation, and evaluation of reform efforts in the classroom, school, district, and community.	All students participate in a variety of decision-making forums—representation of demographic groups, including race or ethnicity, economic status, school success, gender, ability, and language is proportional to the school population. Intentional efforts to include the perspectives of students whose opinions and experiences are different (or in opposition) to the school or larger population are present.	Adults are encouraged to engage students in active learning to share decision-making in the classroom and to uncover students' funds of knowledge and use them to facilitate learning and development. Adults are encouraged to develop opportunities for students to engage in extracurricular activities. Funding and resource allocation, along with professional development activities, support these goals.	School policies are designed to focus attention on the inclusion of youth voice in decision-making, not only at the classroom level, but also at the school and district levels. All adults are expected to participate with youth and develop their own skills. The school actively pursues relationships with other organizations in the community that extend opportunities for engagement and emancipation. Funding and structures ensure the success of these efforts.

Source: Adapted from Shelley Zion and Sheryl Petty, "Student Voices in Urban School and District Improvement: Creating Youth–Adult Partnerships for Student Success and Social Justice," in *Ability, Equity, and Culture: Sustaining Inclusive Urban Education Reform*, ed. ElizabethB. Kozleski and Kathleen King Thorius (New York: Teachers College Press, 2013), 35–62.

Resources to put in place

Money, time, training, and support. These are the four key resources you'll need to have. Money matters: It can be used to secure training and coaching for the teachers who'll support the student voice work. It can be used to pay stipends for planning time for teachers, or for afterschool or summer pay. It can pay students. It can provide funds for research tools, like cameras, recorders, or software for data collection and analysis. It might even pay for pizza and other supplies to support the work. But as much as money matters, time matters more. If you want your teachers and staff to do a great job of engaging with young people, you need to set aside time: time for professional development, time for planning, and time for engaging with students. You'll need to make time to provide support. That means showing up at the teachers' professional development, checking in and listening to young people, and securing time on board or other meeting agendas. As a leader, your presence shows your commitment and support. Finally, don't skip out on the training, both professional development and coaching. Even the best teachers need to revisit the key concepts inherent in providing space to share power and voice with young people, and very few educators receive much training in the intricacies of designing and carrying out research projects or policy asks.

Timelines to implement

Building on the idea of time and support in the previous section, let's talk timelines. Our strongest projects start with getting the adults ready—have your team engage in a book study (of this and our companion book) and in some training sessions. Your choices about curricular changes, afterschool sessions, summer sessions, or inviting student participation on committees will determine who needs to participate in the planning and training, and these choices may influence your timelines. If you want to launch TSV by including students on committees or afterschool clubs at the beginning of the school year, you'll want to spend the prior spring reading and planning and set aside two days in the summer for the final training and preparation. If your plan is summer sessions, begin reading and planning in the fall, with training in the spring. If you are planning on curricular changes to implement CCI in the classroom, you'll want to follow your internal curriculum development process, but be sure to include time for teacher training.

Traps to avoid

The most obvious traps are listed above: the failure to provide adequate time, support, training, or resources. Too often, we've seen districts choose educators who are excellent teachers and assume they don't need training. But sharing power with young people, identifying problems, and conducting research to pose solutions is a whole different skill set and approach than what teachers use in the classroom. So don't skimp on the preparation and training. (We will discuss professional development approaches in chapter 6.)

Another trap pertains to which students you engage in school improvement processes. It is all too common for educators to rely on the same small number of students for leadership opportunities. We have fallen prey to this in our own work, such as when recruiting students to be part of curricular codesign or to speak at conferences. The quickest and easiest move is to find students who have done this before. And yes, you want to be sure some experienced students are part of youth-adult partnership teams; they can mentor and show the way for newer students. But if you're not careful, you will be working in an echo chamber that is not representative of the broad array of experiences of students in your school. Challenge yourself to always ask: Are we inviting the same set of students as before? Are students who struggle at this school part of our discussions about school improvement? Some students will jump at this opportunity; others will need to be invited and encouraged, and they won't agree unless they trust you or key players on the team. We encourage you to build this recruitment process into your timelines so that you can be thoughtful about who is participating.

CONCLUSION

Reflect on the various ways that you include student voice in the work of your school and district, and at what level it falls. Is most of your work happening at the advisor level? Where are there opportunities to deepen the quality of that work—to include more students, or to close the communication loops? Return to the notes you took in chapter 2 about the places where student voice could or should happen. How can you begin to level up to the collaborator or leader levels, if you aren't already doing that? Remember that we want to have student voice at *all* the levels, if we are going to claim to be transformative.

SECTION TWO

TSV Implementation

IN SECTION TWO, we focus on implementation: how TSV works in various settings, including the district, the schools, the classroom, and after school.

We start with chapter 4, which tells the story of student voice programming in Urban School District (USD), our longest running partnership. Building a high-quality student voice program can be challenging—especially if it is expected to be initiated as a fully formed program. The idea of scaling a program over time can thus be more appealing, but it comes with its own challenges. We describe how USD took an intentional approach to scaling by evolving what was a one-off student voice event into a sustained program that supported youth in identifying problems, conducting their own research, and imagining—and proposing—more equitable policy solutions. In describing the process of scaling within the district we highlight the role of the program director in fostering relationships with district administrators and school leaders. Additionally, we describe crucial partnerships outside of the district (with local politicians, community organizations, and university researchers) that led to the evolution of student voice programming with more rigorous research methods and a focus on policy change. Students, in essence, went from being positioned as *cute kids doing cool stuff* to important voices for equity and change in their schools and communities—including changes in policies related to school discipline and school policing. While methodical in its approach, this relationship-based scaling ensured the fidelity of the programming, encouraged adult partners who shielded students from district politics, garnered support for student voice in the community, procured grant funding to support growth, and attracted national recognition. In addressing the merits of a slow scaling of student voice programming we also address the limitations of relationship dependence, including the challenges of growing the program where relationships did not exist, increasing district leadership buy-in, and avoiding staff burnout.

We then move to the foundational work of integrating TSV into the curriculum in content area classes in chapter 5. The narrative of this chapter starts with the story of a middle school teacher who enacted TSV in his literacy class. We then propose a tiered approach to TSV in the classroom, with three levels of adoption: tier 1 emphasizes *sharing power* as a core feature of pedagogy in all classrooms, regardless of content area. In tier 2, a subset of classrooms would bridge student lived experience to academic curriculum through *critical conversations*, even if the assignments and assessments remain tethered to specific predetermined content standards. For this tier, for example, a high school mathematics teacher might have difficulty reorganizing their class into an inquiry-based unit, but they could still practice strategies for sharing power and exploring critical questions using math content. For tier 3, we propose that each grade level ensures that its students are experiencing the full Critical Civic Inquiry (CCI) curriculum

in at least one class. CCI is an approach to classroom pedagogy and curriculum that integrates academic content with a
Youth Participatory Action Research (YPAR) inquiry cycle. We
hope to empower teachers to see curriculum and standards
not as barriers or tensions but as opportunities to connect
academic learning with personally relevant issues and social
justice stances.

The final chapter in this section discusses how to get TSV
started via afterschool clubs or summer sessions. District and
school leaders can use outside of school time (OST) to try out
innovative programs that appeal to student interests but may
not fit into the school day. The beauty of this approach is that
the physical space is already there and sitting unused; moreover, schools have existing infrastructure—because of sports
and other sponsored afterschool activities—to organize the
logistics and budgets of such activities, often in partnership
with nonprofit organizations. We begin by outlining the unique
affordances of OST: students can opt in, educators can be more
responsive to student interests, and curriculum is not beholden
to content standards or end-of-year assessments. Some OST
clubs can be run by teachers, but it is just as common to bring
in AmeriCorps volunteers or representatives from community
organizations with their own funding who are eager to reach
more young people. We highlight programs that have integrated arts and technology to engage young people in self-
expression and critical analysis of their social worlds. There is a
burgeoning field of critical media and technology literacy that
leverages the power of digital media to amplify student voice,
including podcasting, digital storytelling, and photography.
We'll provide examples of student-led project details, as well as
logistical decisions that supported the organization and
running of the sessions for both student researchers and student voice facilitators. Furthermore, we will describe the processes by which youth who were engaged in projects using

summer and afterschool sessions influenced school practices and enhanced the quality of the student experience in their environment, while also building their skills in leadership, literacy, and civic engagement. Finally, we share ideas about how to provide the needed professional development for adults who will facilitate Transformative Student Voice.

FOUR

At the District Level

IN THE MID-2010S, students from Urban School District (USD) were invited to participate in the Student Voice Summit; the event, funded by a local foundation, invited youth from across the country to share their work to address issues in their schools and communities. At the summit, each youth team gave dynamic presentations sharing how they identified their issue of concern and the strategies they took to ameliorate said concern. The following year, the local foundation decided to no longer host the summit, and they handed responsibility for it to USD. In reimagining the event, USD administrators decided it should include only district schools, and they hired a student voice director, Eliana Ramirez, who would be responsible for organizing the event. She came with a social work background and ample experience in community organizing. This skill set aided her in recruiting eight district high schools to participate in the first District Summit.

In the next three years, student voice programming expanded through the district. USD added a yearlong program called Youth Leaders (YL) and training for the educators who facilitated the YL groups. The summit was now the culminating event of YL programming. Through YL, youth learned research and community organizing skills which empowered them to make increasing demands on the district. No longer was the summit an academic exercise; it was now about youth using their voice to impact school and district policy. An early win for YL students was getting the district to agree to change discipline policies for elementary school youth—banning school resource officers from handcuffing students in elementary schools.

The success of youth voice programming was driven by Eliana. She built relationships with principals that helped her expand the number of schools offering YL programs—doubling the number of schools participating over those first three years. She was also respected within district administration, which helped to diffuse tension whenever students became too critical of district policy. For its part, USD created a student voice office within the district structure. This office, run by Eliana, was responsible for all student voice programming across the district.

Eliana also had a wealth of community networks, giving her access to local organizers and politicians who would readily give time to aid students. From these leaders, youth learned about strategies for political organizing and how to partner with community groups. Eliana eventually formed a research-practice partnership with two local universities that led to the refinement of YL curriculum, grant dollars to hire additional personnel, and the further expansion of YL programming to half of all district schools. This is a case of how one school district went about embedding student voice programming into their district structure. Whereas chapter 3 addressed student voice in school improvement, and chapter 5 will look at student voice at the classroom level, here we examine what it looks like for district personnel to run and scale student voice across district schools.

This chapter offers key strategies for how districts can initiate student voice programming. We describe the benefits of housing student voice programming within a district office (or having it led by district personnel), we give a case study on scaling student voice, and we discuss the challenges to implementing student voice and the resources needed for successful implementation. Throughout the chapter we will also revisit examples from YL to highlight how they operate a student voice program within a school district.

THE POWER OF STUDENT VOICE IN DISTRICTS

When school districts commit to student voice, they unlock new possibilities. In particular, they fulfill the democratic potential of schools and gain unique student insights. Schools are essential to preparing young people for democratic participation. In many ways, schools replicate civic systems: schools consist of representational bodies (parent-teacher organizations and student councils), bureaucracies (administrative procedures, compliance, and budgeting), and hierarchies of power. When a school district authentically incorporates student voice in all aspects of their systems, they provide youth with the opportunity to see civics come to life, and young people learn skills that will aid them in civic engagement throughout their lives. We won't rehash all of the specific merits here, but will remind the reader that various scholars noted the academic and social-emotional benefits of students engaging in action-oriented civics.[1] We also share below a reflection from Derek White, a YL teacher, describing how he has witnessed empowerment from YL participants.

DEREK WHITE, YL TEACHER, USD

 We've noticed a lot of our students speaking at board meetings...And that first [school board] meeting I think about twenty students spoke, most of whom were affiliated with [YL]. And so I feel like it's kind of giving, it's helping students feel empowered, maybe giving them permission like, "I can speak at board meetings;...I can say what's on my mind; I can express my feelings and what's happened to me, or what I've seen in our school system so far." So we've definitely noticed, like, students feeling more empowered to express themselves...The other effects that occurred after that first meeting, that first board meeting, that when they presented, a number of teachers who heard contacted us right away for various things, from "How do my students get involved?" to "Can your students come talk to my class?"

Just as important as the civic learning it provides, student voice is also a way for schools to access the unique insights of youth. Students have an insider perspective into schools to which adult administrators are not privy. On a campus tour years ago, a group of students showed Ben and Carlos blind spots in the school's corridors. These blind spots were not visible on school cameras, nor were they patrolled by staff, and the students said that these were spots where incidents of campus violence took place. In an example such as this, the inclusion of student voice in safety planning might lead to better ways to address both physical and metaphorical blind spots.

Students from marginalized backgrounds, specifically students of color and queer students, possess insights about school operations that might not be readily available to school leaders of majority groups.[2] In a recent conversation with community leaders, Carlos learned of an underground network of information sharing for students of color at a local school. These youth shared with each other which teachers and administrators were welcoming and supportive of students of color and what specific policies students could cite when advocating for themselves. These youth also shared the names of educators they felt were biased or should otherwise be avoided. By incorporating the voices of marginalized students into school systems, educators can learn of, and ultimately ameliorate, inequities.

RELATIONSHIPS MATTER

In chapter 2, we introduced the idea of scaling vertically and horizontally. In USD's scaling of YL, these notions of vertical and horizontal scaling were definitely driving efforts. On the horizontal scale, YL sought to expand programming to new schools, and on the vertical scale, YL wanted to foster a deeper commitment to TSV among district administrators. These goals were set so that YL would be available to more students across the district. Simultaneously, training would be provided to YL teachers to strengthen their understanding of youth voice, action civics, and research methods. Additionally, administrators would seek to incorporate youth voice in district policy and improvement plans.

A key to this scaling process was relationships. The YL director relied on building relationships with district administration and principals, which took time. Potential school sites for expansion came from previously held relationships, through Eliana knowing a principal personally or professionally, or through community recommendations—a mutual relationship or someone vouching for a principal. The logic behind this was to ensure that the principal of a given site was committed to student voice and YL programming. Each site was required to have a coach who would work with the student voice team at their school, and the principal would meet with youth to hear their policy proposals. It would often take multiple meetings to assure alignment of vision between new sites and YL staff. A strength of this approach was the requirement for some degree of commitment from sites to uphold the values of YL and engage young people in decision-making. Another benefit was scaling with depth—schools that took on YL had a greater degree of commitment, but if things were not going as desired, Eliana had enough of a connection with the principals to be able to have frank discussions.

A downside was that this led to a slower approach to scaling, with only two or three new schools being brought on yearly. It was also difficult to expand programming to schools where previous relationships did not exist. A change in school leadership often presented another challenge: City Park High School, for example, had developed a strong YL team, but a new principal came in and was not interested in continuing the YL program. Despite students pushing for a team, and Eliana attempting to persuade her, the principal would not reconsider. Ultimately, it was only due to pressure from the superintendent that YL programming returned to City Park—demonstrating the importance of having the support of upper-level administrators.

Though new school sites were being added to YL, the budget from USD did not keep pace. The two YL staff people, a director and a program coordinator, were being asked to expand offerings. At this point YL programming included student teams at nearly twenty high schools, a training group for team coaches, a superintendent advisory board, an all-district team focused on Black and Latine students, and the District Summit event. Running a program of this size (see figure 4.1) was challenging for a staff of two. The horizontal aspect of scaling was progressing well, but budget and support from the district was not keeping pace.

This is not to say that the district did not contribute; they did create an office for student voice with two staff people and a small budget for programming. Additionally, high-level district administrators, including the superintendent, frequently

FIGURE 4.1 **YL program structure**

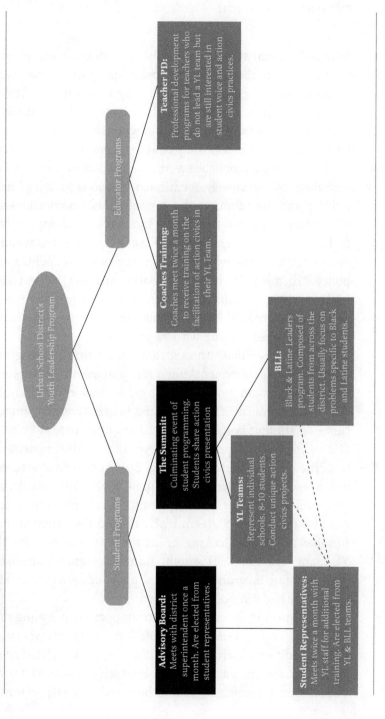

Urban School District's
Youth Leadership Program

Educator Programs

Student Programs

Teacher PD:
Professional development programs for teachers who do not lead a YL team but are still interested in student voice and action civics practices.

Coaches Training:
Coaches meet twice a month to receive training on the facilitation of action civics in their YL Team.

The Summit:
Culminating event of student programming. Students share action civics presentation

BLL:
Black & Latine Leaders program. Composed of students from across the district. Usually focus on problems specific to Black and Latine students.

YL Teams:
Represent individual schools. 8–10 students. Conduct unique action civics projects.

Advisory Board:
Meets with district superintendent once a month. Are elected from student representatives.

Student Representatives:
Meets twice a month with YL staff for additional training. Are elected from YL & BLL teams.

attended student voice events to listen to students and provide youth with feedback on their policy proposals—this access to high-level administrators is a major benefit of district-embedded student voice. It is much easier for district officials to ignore outside advocacy groups, but when district officials hear from their own students, they tend to be more receptive. A few student-generated policies were even adopted districtwide, including the previously mentioned revisions to disciplinary policies and the adoption of a gender studies curriculum—we will speak more about this later in the chapter. The opportunity to learn about district policymaking was also a tremendous benefit for students, who learned to navigate adult politics and policy structures. The district officials would also seek out feedback from YL students when new policies or programs were being considered. The main challenge, though, was district funding not keeping pace with YL growth.

Fortunately, Eliana, through a mutual contact, met a group of university researchers. After a series of meetings and some collaborations on youth trainings, it was clear that the researchers and the YL team shared values about the importance of student voice, a desire to amplify student voice in USD, and a hope to provide more youth with the opportunity to participate in YL programming. Based on these shared values, a research-practice partnership (RPP) was formed with the two local universities. The two teams collaborated on a curriculum to support YL team teachers, and they applied for a number of grants. Seeking grant funding was new for the YL team. Though USD sought numerous grants annually, the idea of using grant dollars to support or even include student voice had not been considered.

One grant in specific aimed to support YL in scaling programming through USD. The funds from this grant were used to hire additional staff for YL, conduct research on YL student outcomes, and increase the number of schools with YL teams. The RPP team (university researchers and YL staff) presented at district-led professional development sessions for teachers, met with district leaders, and presented to the USD school board. Research outcomes were shared widely, showing the positive impact on YL students' academic and social-emotional growth, all in the hopes of attracting interest from potential school sites. These efforts did raise the profile of YL locally and within the national youth voice community of practitioners and scholars. Over the period of this grant, additional schools were brought on. Programming was available at nearly 80 percent of district-run schools by the end of the grant cycle, but was not at the lofty mark of 100 percent participation that the RPP had hoped. Alas, YL was never able to shake the relational approach to scaling—partially because the district never moved to make student voice central to its mission and operation. Granted there were some major changes within USD during these grant years (including leadership changes, a teacher strike, and COVID-19), but as long as the school leaders viewed student voice programming as optional, a relational approach was almost a necessity. Those sites that were brought on were typically those where previous relationships existed or where meetings yielded commitments to YL values.

Similarly, further integration of student voice into USD proved challenging. When district administrators left, the process of relationship building had to begin anew. A new superintendent, for example, had to be introduced to YL programming and its benefits. This led to the student voice office being shifted from one area of the district structure to another. Although this was less than optimal, the fact that they were part of the district meant that they retained access to influence. An outside youth voice organization might find themselves shut out of a district entirely when leadership changes occur. USD continues to espouse a commitment to student voice in general and to YL specifically. The superintendent has recently asked the YL director to develop a new plan to expand programming to all district schools. Using the lessons learned from previous attempts, the YL director is seeking to first ensure vertical scaling before expanding horizontally.

CHALLENGES

Establishing a new educational program in a public school system can be challenging. However, creating a TSV program can be particularly difficult, especially because TSV challenges power relationships and established norms. In this section, we will explore policies and practices that can limit the effective implementation of TSV in a district. We will examine limits to participation, hierarchies of power, symbolic voice, and interest alignment. We will also share examples of how YL has skirted these issues.

Limits to Participation

Student voice programs—those that highlight the lived experiences of students, that seek power sharing between youth and adults, and that give youth an authentic say in school policies and practices (not student councils or student advisory boards)—are rare within school districts, particularly urban districts.[3] When these programs do exist, there are often limits on who gets to participate, usually based on grade point average and disciplinary record.[4] An unfortunate side effect of this is that only a select few students get the opportunity to engage in the powerful experience of action civics, participatory action research, and learning about adult political spheres.

When participation in TSV is limited to high-achieving students, the perspectives of a youth voice team are colored by the experiences of those for whom school is already working. High-achieving students have figured out how to succeed within its existing structures. What is more, high-achieving students have values that are generally aligned with those of school leaders.[5] This can lead to an echo chamber, where high-achieving students reinforce the values and perspectives of school leadership. Lost are the critical insights of those for whom school is *not* working.

Students who are struggling academically, who have experienced disciplinary sanctions, or who are marginally engaged (coming to school but not involved in extracurriculars, for example) have unique insights into schools. Their experiences can illuminate where school services are falling short: things like gaps in services, discriminatory policies, and lack of access might come to light. These critical insights are only possible when all students are engaged.

YL does not impose any limits to student participation. This can be a point of contention with some school leaders. The belief is often that if a student is struggling academically, they should not be given the privilege of engaging in an extracurricular activity, or that struggling students should focus on academics alone. This discussion is a nonstarter; for a school to offer YL programming they are not allowed to put up barriers to participation based on GPA.

What we have found in our own research is that youth who engage in student voice programming experience academic and social-emotional gains, including perceived relevance of school and increased self-efficacy. Our contention is that engagement in youth voice actually inspires youth to do better academically by making their learning relevant to their lives and to become more engaged in school by showing how their voice can impact school policies. Additionally, participating in youth voice groups provides students with a community of peers and access to a teacher who is more student-centered, providing the potential to engage a student who might be otherwise on the margins of school or struggling academically.

Adult Hierarchies

When people ask Carlos what he thinks is the hardest part of implementing TSV in schools, his answer is: getting adults to share power with youth. Most school leaders we have met endorse the value of student voice, but when we push for examples of how they engage students in decision-making, the room goes quiet. It can be challenging for educators to share power with youth; in many cases it goes against their educational training and years of experience.

Unfortunately, hierarchies of power are an established part of American schools.[6] In most schools, youth have little to no power over major decisions; instead, policies and practices are imposed on students.[7] This reality is grounded in adultism—the ideology that adults are superior, and that they are entitled to make decisions on behalf of youth.[8]

Hierarchies of power and adultism are incompatible with TSV. As we have described in chapter 1, TSV requires sustained partnerships between youth and adults where youth have an authentic say in school policies and practices. For this to be possible, adults must believe in the ability of youth and believe that they are capable partners who are able to contribute to the mission of schools. Adults must also share power with students to give youth a say on school policy and procedures.

One major benefit of the relational-based scaling approach used by YL was the ability to only include schools where leaders showed readiness to act as partners to youth. The YL director frequently screened out potential adult collaborators who would not be partners with youth. While there are lessons that can be learned from engaging opposition, interactions are more beneficial and fulfilling for students when adults support student voice. As much as there was a desire for all students to have access to student voice programming, YL was unwilling to start a team at a school that did not have supportive leadership. This protected the fidelity of programming, ensuring that student voice would not be an academic exercise or possibly even disempowering for youth.

Symbolic Voice

When we asked district leaders about what student voice looks like in their schools, they gave examples like having a student council or including a student representative on committees. This type of student voice is symbolic—youth have a position on school-related boards, but no real say in school policy.[9] Using the example of the student council, they might have some authority to decide on the themes of dances or what mascot a school might adopt, for example, but neither of these decisions have any meaningful impact on the functioning of a school. In the example of a student representative or student board member, administrative personnel might look to these representatives for feedback on policies. This gives the illusion of voice—students give feedback but are not able to collaborate or initiate policy. This illusion gets in the way of actually implementing student voice in a district; leaders see these examples as authentic engagement in voice, giving them a sense of accomplishment. In reality there are no authentic partnerships, and the student contribution is, at best, feedback.

The YL director for USD would get frequent requests from district administrators and community organizations looking to present their ideas to the YL participants. In many cases, these organizations sought endorsements from youth, inviting them to speak on behalf of certain policies. In one case, a school board member invited YL participants to speak in support of a policy she was proposing to the board. Two YL teams had worked on similar policies and had consulted with her previously. But the board member chose not to collaborate with these youth; instead she sought the appearance of student voice—youth endorsing her proposal—as opposed to authentic partnership.

To avoid symbolic voice, school districts can position youth as contributors to policy (look back to some of the examples in chapter 3). TSV provides a model for this, with students investigating an issue and proposing a policy solution. Beyond this, district leaders can partner with youth to help operationalize these policy suggestions. The opportunity to collaborate with adults and get firsthand experience will provide unique and powerful civic learning experiences for students.

Interest Alignment

Interest alignment is what happens when school leaders only promote student voice initiatives that align with administrative interests. Both Jerusha Conner and Gerry Czerniawski described how student voice initiatives that supported the priorities of school leaders were more likely to be endorsed by school administration.[10] Student voice initiatives that went against administration interests, however, were more likely to be dismissed.

Interest alignment can be a challenge for implementing student voice at the district level, because administrators are quick to point to examples where the alignment existed and youth initiatives were promoted. This gives school leaders and district officials the impression that they are responsive to youth voice in their district, when in reality, they are only promoting student policies that support adult interests.

To avoid this trap, it is important to bring attention to the full number of proposals brought forth or initiated by students. How many of these were enacted? Of those that were enacted, how many directly aligned with existing initiatives or district priorities? It is also wise to consider which student groups are bringing forward successful voice initiatives. Specifically consider the schools they come from; their gender, race, or ethnicity; and their socioeconomic status. It is often the case that students from majority backgrounds are more heard, perhaps because their values more closely align with the people who lead school districts.

In our work with USD we often came across officials who discussed the district's new gender studies course as an example of how they were responsive to student voice. These administrators almost uniformly shared how the course idea was initiated by a group of high school students. They talked about how these students met with their principal, the district's director of social studies curriculum, the superintendent, and the school board, winning over these administrators along the way with their rationale for the course. Though this was indeed a powerful example, it was the only example of an adopted student voice proposal that USD officials could name. Never mind that the state social studies standards had changed the previous year and required ethnic studies, gender studies, and queer studies to be incorporated into high school curriculums. It is also worth noting that a few YL teams had proposed an ethnic studies curriculum to the district in the past, but those policies were not adopted. It was not until the interests of students aligned with the priorities of the district that a gender studies course was created.

As we have mentioned previously, scaling a program is always challenging.

MEADOW BLACKWELL, PRINCIPAL, JOHN LEWIS HIGH SCHOOL

 I think having [Eliana] and a team of students and principals maybe just speak to schools that do not have student leadership, speak to both the pros and the cons because you got to speak to both. And when you speak to the cons, you can speak to how a principal has overcome those, and why it's important to have student leadership, will probably help a principal to truly understand the benefits of having student leadership in the building.

I think when we speak to principals and you're not willing to talk about the challenges—if you just go into a building and you speak to the principals about all of the positives, you leave a principal to say, "No. There—no. There's something else to be said here." But if you're honest and you say, "There's both positives or—and growth opportunities here, but here are some ways that we have overcome the growth opportunities." I'm not going to lie. This was difficult. Here's some—we've butt heads on some occasions. Here's some examples of how we didn't see or how we didn't agree, but here's why. But this is how we overcame that, and this is how we worked together, and here's the outcome from us working together . . .

And when we work together and we put our heads together, and we have the perspective of students that are going through life right now, and you have the perspective of adults, who have, like we say, been there, done that, we have all the experience—but when you put all of those perspectives together, you get greatness. You don't get stuck in a rut. You're not doing the same old, same old. You get innovative ideas that affect all stakeholders, and you get greatness that everyone can buy into.

And I think when you have a school that can hear both sides, most people are more apt to jump on board to have student leadership in their building. But I think they need to hear both sides. They need to hear that there's going to be some difficult conversations on both sides. They need to hear, "Students, you're not going to win all the time. Principal, leadership, you're not going to win all the time," because that's the truth. But we're going to agree to disagree, we're going to come together on some things, and we're going to make greatness happen.

SUGGESTIONS FOR SUCCESS

Successfully implementing student voice within a school district requires commitments from school leaders and district officials. In our work with YL we noted that this commitment is facilitated by adults who are willing to advocate for youth voice programming and be mentors for students. There must also be some tolerance and anticipation of conflict, as student voice will inevitably clash with district policy. In the subsequent section we will address these points as well as the need for district-level support for student voice, and how multiyear programming can advance student learning.

District Leadership

In large districts

The idea of a dedicated student voice office in the district might be somewhat novel to readers. This is because student voice typically exists at the classroom level in most schools (we provide examples in chapter 5). Usually it is one teacher who pushes student voice in their school. What a district office can do is unify these lone wolf advocates, give them a sense of community, provide training, and align student voice with district priorities.

Within USD, the YL program was initially housed in the office for postsecondary programming—the office dedicated to promoting college and career preparation. This departmental home was advantageous, as it increased the visibility of YL within the district; they were frequently introduced along with programs such as SAT test prep and financial aid workshops. It also made for a beneficial association between postsecondary readiness and YL's action civics training. From a pragmatic standpoint, this home also protected YL from budget cuts, since district leaders tended to view postsecondary programs as essential to student success. Lastly, what educator would refuse a meeting from someone in postsecondary programming?

In later years, YL moved to the office of culturally responsive curriculum, but this was short-lived, because there was little alignment between YL and other programs in this area.

Ultimately the office was placed directly under the superintendent. Being housed in the superintendent's office was seen as a positive, and the move was meant to increase visibility of the program throughout the district and facilitate access to high-level administrators. In reality, the move did not lead to more youth policies being adopted.

It is hard to say that there is the perfect home for TSV programs within a district; there are tradeoffs with any placement. In our team discussions we have mused about where we would place a TSV program. Generally, we like a home associated with curriculum so that TSV is centered in the student experiences. A home in social studies curriculum can make sense, given the civics lens of TSV, but we have also seen TSV work in writing and other humanities (see some of the examples in chapter 5). Carlos likes TSV in postsecondary and college readiness, thinking that TSV leads to civics education, which is an essential component of adult life. Wherever your district ultimately decides to house TSV, what is important is that there is commitment to student voice as part of your mission and practices, and that sufficient resources are given to the program so that it will thrive.

In smaller districts

The idea of a committed office of student voice might be more challenging for smaller districts that do not have the staff or resources of their larger counterparts. In this case, having a leader at the district level who is responsible for programming is an appropriate alternative. We recommend that the leader be someone in the area of curriculum instruction. If the goal is to spread student voice in the district, a leader with a curriculum and instruction background will have the ear of district administration and teachers. Furthermore, they will have the ability to impact district policies and practices so that student voice is better incorporated.

Picking the right leader

The right student voice leader is passionate about student voice, skilled in relationship building, and capable of navigating district politics. Being a director of student voice in a school district requires a unique skill set—having a solid background in the theory and practice of TSV, but also the ability to manage and lead within an educational system. It is rare to find a candidate who possesses both, as most youth voice organizers operate outside of school systems and most district leaders do not have experience with TSV programs.

In the case of USD, they brought in a YL director who had experience in youth and community organizing. Though she did not have as much experience in educational administration, she brought a passion for the work and a wealth of community connections. Her passion endeared her to students and educators who were interested in student voice. Her connections helped her to network within the district, form relationships across offices, and become a respected leader. With time, she became knowledgeable in navigating district politics, knowing when she could make demands of district leaders and when a more collaborative approach was necessary, which was useful in securing resources or helping students with their policy asks. Though finding the right person to lead student voice efforts in a district might be challenging, it is essential to find a person with the right skills and disposition.

Adult Mentors

As we mentioned earlier in the chapter, part of the power of TSV in a school district is the ability to work directly with adult decision-makers. Though mentoring and partnering with youth might sound straightforward, especially for educators, in reality it can be difficult. Most classrooms are run in a didactic fashion, with teachers in firm control of instruction. In his writing, Ben has described the art of mentoring youth through student voice.[11] A good adult mentor provides enough support to youth so they don't flounder but gives them enough space so they can learn through experience. Unfortunately, a lack of training in this art often leads to adult mentors adopting strategies that go against the principles of student voice.[12] If you are interested in learning more about how to teach Transformative Student Voice, we recommend reading the companion volume to this text.[13]

As YL grew, there was a need to train more educators on leading youth voice groups. To meet that need, YL developed an educator training component. This group met twice monthly and was intended to provide educators with training on the student voice curriculum. The group was also an opportunity for teachers to share tips on what was working and where they needed support. When YL partnered with the university researchers, additional resources were dedicated to teacher training. Grant funding allowed YL to hire a full-time coordinator for teacher education, who collaborated with one of the university researchers to develop more robust educator training. This included formalizing the TSV curriculum that YL used and bringing in specific training for teachers on root cause analysis, research, and policy development. The success of this training led YL to offer student voice training during USD professional development meetings and, eventually, a yearlong professional development course for teachers outside of YL who were interested in implementing TSV principles in their classroom.

Many of the educators who participated in these meetings (either the YL group or the professional development group) philosophically endorsed student voice, but the training provided them with the knowledge and skill set to be good adult mentors. We also heard from educators how it was beneficial to collaborate with others who were implementing TSV. Each of these educators was the only person in their building leading this type of work, so getting together with others allowed them space for consultation and collaboration.

Though these teachers exhibited a range of styles in their mentorship, with some being more directive and others allowing students to lead, the group training ensured that these educators were more deliberate about how they supported their students.

Anticipate Conflict

When students claim voice within school systems, conflict is likely to ensue. Through TSV, youth develop critical thinking skills and efficacy in sociopolitical action. At some point, these youth will turn their gaze toward school systems and district practices. This will likely lead to critiques of the system and calls for change. While there is great benefit from youth sharing insider perspectives about where schools might not be serving them, some school leaders will likely feel threatened by these critiques.

A knee-jerk reaction from some educators will be to dismiss student concerns or, worse yet, to end student voice programming. By anticipating conflict, which we discuss further in chapter 7, you prepare yourself as a district leader for the eventuality that students will form a critique of schools and the district. Again, we encourage you to view these critiques as unique stakeholder feedback that allows the district to better serve students.

Often these critiques will be presented passionately by youth. Avoid the temptation to see this passion as anger. Viewing it as anger makes you more likely to get defensive or to dismiss the message behind that passion. Also resist the temptation to rationalize or provide explanations for district policy and practice. Instead, be a listening ear; students want to be heard. Jumping to explaining without first listening can be viewed as being dismissive. You don't have to agree with the critique or enjoy receiving it, but by truly listening to the concerns of youth you can diffuse tensions and prepare a space for collaboration.

Occasionally students will not go through identified channels when presenting their critiques or policy solutions. This might include using social media or staging unauthorized protests. Realize that students are not versed in adult politics, might be ignorant of district feedback processes, are at an age where they might be impatient, and are often from communities that are typically marginalized by school and governmental systems. You must resist the temptation to ignore the message because it did not come through proper channels. A reframe is that the students of your district are so empowered that they are using all avenues available to them to have their voices be heard. Again, being willing to listen will go a long way toward developing trust and acquiring stakeholder feedback.

On a number of occasions, YL youth have ruffled the feathers of USD leadership. In most of these cases it was Eliana who stepped in to smooth things out. In some cases, she worked with the young people to help them think about their approach in advocating for change, and she helped the students to consider alternative ways to have their voice heard. In other cases, she reached out to district personnel who were the target of students' call for change, helping them understand the context and rationale for the youths' approach. This ability to engage administrators and youth usually helped the YL director de-escalate tensions. This again points to the importance of having a student voice director who is equally skilled in working with youth and navigating school systems.

Multiyear Engagement

When student voice exists in schools, it is typically for shorter-term engagements. At best, youth might get a yearlong experience, but in some cases, it is only a semester—and we have worked with teachers who have designed six-week modules. We will be the first to advocate that any student voice experiences are better than none at all, but the potential of TSV gets unlocked with multiyear experiences for youth.

In our own research we have documented how shorter experiences with student voice can serve as a protective factor for youth of color.[14] In a semester-long setting, students who participated in student voice programming maintained their efficacy and ethnic identity, whereas those in the comparison group experienced losses in these areas. In subsequent studies we found a direct relationship between years of student voice participation and engagement in political action.[15] We have also documented how teachers have used multiyear engagement as a way to increase leadership opportunities for youth and as a form of peer mentoring.[16] In that classroom, the teacher positioned students with multiple years of experience as leaders. In one instance, a senior student was in charge of leading a group of students in an activity while the teacher worked with a more novice group of students on the basics of student voice work. Another fascinating aspect of this classroom was the way more senior students mentored younger students to take on leadership roles. This aided the continuity of this group's student voice work. Instead of having to start from ground zero every year, students in this group were able to build off the previous years' work, and there was a cadre of students with historical knowledge to lead the group.

The main takeaway here is that when students have the opportunity to participate in longer terms of engagement with TSV, student outcomes—particularly for students from marginalized backgrounds—improve. Thus, when planning for a district-based student voice program, it would be wise to consider designing the program to provide multiyear engagement opportunities for youth.

YL has a number of structures that encourage multiyear engagement. Most students begin their YL involvement on a school-based team. Each team then elects two to four students to serve as their team representatives. Representatives are usually in their second or third year of involvement with YL. The representatives attend cross-district meetings twice a month and receive additional training on action research and policymaking. These representatives are responsible for taking this training back to their school-based teams. A smaller subset of representatives are then elected to the executive board of YL. These are usually students in their third or fourth year of YL involvement. The executive board helps plan out YL activities for the year and are often called upon to work with USD officials, providing feedback on district initiatives. From this model, the reader can see how students with multiple years of engagement in YL are encouraged to take on increasing responsibility, thus growing their leadership and advocacy skills.

LEVELING UP

Throughout this chapter we have discussed what embedding TSV in a district can look like and used YL as an example. However, USD has yet to unlock the full potential of student voice, due largely to limited vertical integration. So what would it look like for TSV to be fully integrated into a school district? In this section we describe what a more intentional integration of student voice at the district level might look like.

An essential component to TSV success at a district level is buy-in by district leaders. The district superintendent, curriculum coordinator, student life coordinator, and other high-ranking staff should appreciate the contributions of student voice and be trained in practices to facilitate TSV in schools and across the district. Part of this commitment should be an agreement to regularly—at least twice an academic year—meet with youth voice leaders, authentically listening to their concerns and providing supportive feedback. Below is a reflection from the chief strategy officer for USD, who reinforces the importance of district follow-through on student voice demands.

PETER BROWN, CHIEF STRATEGY OFFICER, USD

 Well, now you put these students on the stage, and they've elevated this thing. And the superintendent or the deputy superintendent or board members are sitting there, and community partners are sitting there. And all this is going out publicly, and it's like, you better freaking pay attention. You've given voice to this, and people should be asking what we're doing about it, if we're doing something about it, not just our students asking but a more comprehensive audience for that. So I do think those are key.

District buy-in goes beyond espousing the value of youth input, it necessitates policies and practices that require student voice in matters of curriculum, assessment, budget, discipline, and improvement. Again, we are not talking about symbolic participation on these boards, but rather having students as full voting members, with the opportunity to develop policy both individually and collaboratively with other committee members. To increase accountability to authentic integration, we recommend that board committees conduct an annual audit to examine the number of student voice policies proposed and adopted. This accounting will make it clear if the district and its committees are indeed heeding student voice.

A solid mandate on TSV would also require schools within the district to implement student voice. What this looks like will differ based on grade level (in chapter 5 we will discuss what TSV might look like at a single school site). Let's also be clear that commitment to TSV requires an adequate budget for programming. It will take financial resources to pay adult coaches (especially if TSV duties are on top of their usual roles as educators) and to support student skill development (consider things like attending youth conferences or purchasing technology to support research).

The appointment of a student voice coordinator is essential. As we noted above, this might be a single person or an office, depending on the size of your district. The qualities of a good student voice coordinator were described above, but here we want to reinforce that it is the responsibility of this coordinator to facilitate adult training for district leaders, school leaders, and teachers. For TSV to be successful, adults must be ready to collaborate and work with youth. Additionally, the student voice coordinator would be responsible for overseeing TSV work with students. In the ideal model, this coordinator is not running student programs (note this is a little different than what YL does); instead, those TSV learning opportunities are embedded in the district curriculum. The coordinator then would help recruit and train teachers to deliver said curriculum. It would also be the coordinator's responsibility to oversee the assessment of TSV and the fidelity of implementation—ensuring that student voice does not become watered down and achieves its full potential. The coordinator might, however, provide more advanced training to more senior students, particularly those who might staff positions on district boards. Being an adult ally to those students in leadership roles will go a long way toward helping these youth understand and navigate the adult politics of school bureaucracy.

CONCLUSION

In describing the process of horizontal scaling within the district, we highlighted the role of the program director in fostering relationships with district administrators and school leaders. Additionally, we describe the evolution of student voice programming with more focus on policy change. While methodical in its approach, this relationship-based scaling ensured the fidelity of the programming, encouraged adult partners who shielded students from district politics, garnered support for student voice in the community, procured grant funding to support growth, and attracted national recognition. In addressing the merits of a slow scaling of student voice programming, we also address the limitations of relationship dependence, including the challenges of growing the program where relationships did not exist and increasing district leadership buy-in. We also provided the reader with roadblocks to be aware of and strategies for successful implementation. Through this chapter we highlighted the strategies that one student voice program used to implement TSV in a school district setting.

FIVE

In the Classroom and Curriculum

with Dane Stickney

THE ACADEMIC CLASSROOM can be either the easiest or the most difficult setting in which to integrate Transformative Student Voice. The easy part is if we are talking about just one teacher's classroom. One motivated and skilled teacher can do a lot to shape their classroom norms and practices. Over the years we have worked with many valiant—but isolated—teachers who lead transformative work with their students, leading to greater student engagement and academic learning.[1] Other studies have described similar cases where teachers integrated student-centered participatory action research into math, science, literacy, and civics.[2]

The greater challenge comes when we explore what it means for a school or district to infuse TSV across multiple teachers and classrooms. Teachers bring a wide set of assumptions and beliefs about student voice and agency. Some teachers may be comfortable taking risks with their students, others may need more support. Moreover, different subjects place different content demands on students and teachers;

while literacy or statistics are well-suited to participatory action research, chemistry or calculus are less so.

Although challenging, a whole-school approach to TSV across the curriculum brings great reward. What if students could confidently walk into the building knowing that, as they moved through the day, their classrooms would be spaces where their opinions mattered and they felt seen by their teacher? What if, rather than asking themselves what the point was of a specific lesson or assignment, they could see its relevance to their everyday lives and aspirations? What if, instead of seeking the most efficient way to "do school" in each class, students felt inspired to challenge themselves and go deep in their learning?

This chapter offers a strategy and examples to make those scenarios more possible. It is especially geared toward chief academic officers, academic department directors, directors of professional development, and curriculum coordinators. We open with a case example describing what TSV can look like when a teacher engages their students in a yearlong project. Then we step back to describe a tiered approach to the TSV curriculum, starting with a foundation of the most widely adopted practices and moving to those that would be integrated in a subset of classrooms. While dreaming big, we are not naive. We name challenges and barriers throughout so you can design in anticipation of them.

TRANSFORMATIVE STUDENT VOICE IN THE CLASSROOM AND CURRICULUM

Addressing Immigration Rights in a Literacy Class

College pennants hang on the walls of a charter middle school and shout the names of universities far out of state. "HARVARD," reads one in big, block letters. "MICHIGAN," "TEXAS," "WILLIAM & MARY." The charter school has gone all-in on college. Students start the day by gathering in a large room the school has named "the Quad"—an homage to the open areas on college campuses. The principal—a white woman who attended a prestigious university in the intermountain west—leads a daily chant: "Why are we here?" she asks. "To strive for college!" respond the 350 students, roughly 95 percent of whom identify as Latine and qualify for free or reduced-price lunch.

After the all-school gathering, one student, a sixth-grader named Jorge, makes his way to his literacy classroom, which is named for Tulane University. He looks agitated, which isn't typical for him, given that he's one of the stronger students in the class. Not realizing that Jorge is about to redirect the class down a yearlong path of critique, inquiry, and action, his teacher asks what's wrong. "Mister," Jorge says, in front of the rest of his classmates, "I hate saying the college thing every day." His writing teacher (a white man who grew up in Nebraska), still confused, asks why. Jorge explains that he's undocumented. His mother brought him and his siblings across the US-Mexico border when Jorge was a small child. Money is tight. Regardless of how well he does in school, Jorge says, they won't be able to afford college. Jorge isn't sure if it's legal for undocumented youth to go to college in the United States.

Jorge's comments inspire his classmates to speak up. They ask questions about college access for undocumented students. After learning that, in their state, undocumented students pay international tuition rates for state-funded college, they express anger that undocumented students, who make up roughly 60 percent of the school's enrollment, have a tougher path to college than their US-born classmates. They question the school's college-centric focus given the contradictions with state and national legislation.

Jorge's teacher, Dane Stickney, had the wisdom to see this interaction as a spark for further inquiry and action. Stickney, working with Critical Civic Inquiry curriculum resources, guided students through a process of analyzing themselves, looking critically at their school experiences, and arguing for equitable change. Throughout the year, students wrote narratives about their experiences with documentation, deportation, and discrimination. They researched state and national law pertaining to undocumented student access to college. That research pointed to what the students believed was an egregious gap in state law. Even if a student went to public school in the state for their entire academic career, they would have to pay international tuition rates at an in-state public university, which rivaled the most expensive private universities.

Students unanimously decided to take action to fix the problem. After learning of pending state legislation that would address the injustice, they identified on-the-fence legislators to whom they should address their arguments. They researched the biographies of these legislators to gather insight that would make their letters as persuasive as possible. (Remember, this was a literacy class.)

Although it might appear that this problem was primarily the domain of state policy, it had important repercussions for school culture. Students wanted to address the fact that the school promoted a college-going message but did not educate students about the consequences of immigration status for access to college. In addition to writing their letters, students also demanded that the school form an undocumented student task force to assess how the school served immigrant students. The youth had a say in the adult members of that group. They also worked with teachers to establish a scholarship for undocumented students. A number of teachers and staff signed up for monthly contributions. Years later, Jorge was one of the scholarship's first awardees.[3]

The immigrant rights project is a comprehensive example of Transformative Student Voice in the classroom. It spanned most of the year and moved from initial conversations about the issue, to systematic research, to action for policy change. But not everyone can or should do the comprehensive version. For example, some content areas may not permit this kind of open-ended, inquiry-driven approach to curriculum. Some teachers may be less confident in their ability to facilitate problem-based learning. And from the standpoint of the student, we're not sure if it is desirable for every class to be engaging in participatory action research, insofar as it would generate countless change recommendations and likely create some redundancy for students.

THE TIERED APPROACH TO TSV CLASSROOMS

Given these considerations, we recommend a tiered approach, called TSV in the classroom, summarized in figure 5.1. In the tiered approach, all classes would practice some aspects, and a subset would go further. Tier 1 emphasizes *sharing power* as a core feature of pedagogy in all classrooms, regardless of content area. In tier 2, some classrooms would bridge students' lived experience to academic curriculum through *critical conversations*, even if the assignments and assessments remain tethered to specific predetermined content standards. For tier 3, we propose that each grade level ensures that its students are experiencing the full *Critical Civic Inquiry* curriculum in one class. We elaborate on each of these below.

Tier 1: Sharing Power

Transformative Student Voice starts with relationships. Most students will be reluctant to speak up if they do not

FIGURE 5.1   **Sharing power in the classroom**

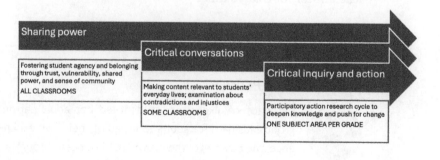

Sharing Power in the Classroom

feel seen and respected in the classroom. Developing trust and safety is just as important for high schoolers as it is in elementary school. Research from a variety of fields—including neuroscience, social and emotional learning, and trauma-informed care—all converge on the necessity of trust, belonging, and community as building blocks of a learning environment.[4]

Our work with TSV embraces this relational approach and extends it to look critically at issues of power and adultism between students and teachers. Humanizing practices in a TSV classroom come to life when teachers view their students as partners in the education journey and share power accordingly. It means partnerships, not paternalism. Educators locate themselves for their students. When teachers and students are vulnerable with each other, they can begin to chip away at assumed hierarchies of power. Because such efforts counter business as usual in American public schools, this process requires intentional practice and learning by teachers and students. In this section, we share brief explanations of each practice to give you a sense of what is included. Our companion book, *Transformative Student Voice for Teachers: A Guide to Classroom Action*, shares more in-depth guidance and examples that show how teachers can share power in the classroom. The teacher whose story began this chapter, Dane Stickney, is the lead author for that volume.

DEREK WHITE, HIGH SCHOOL TEACHER (ON SHARING POWER)

On a lot of, like, other student-led but adult partner groups, it's hard for adults to let go of their own experience, their own ego, their own, "But I've been through all this, you should know about this," and just let the students do their thing. And so, yeah, it's been hard for me ... I have these ideas about what could be in this [project]. I had to bite my tongue ... I don't think any adults have tried to co-opt it ... but it's just like, maybe trying to cultivate them too much, whereas it's like, "No. Let them go do their thing, it'll be all right."

Leadership roles for students

This is perhaps the lowest-hanging fruit of the TSV classroom. One of the most direct ways to reinforce a sense of shared power is to create and scaffold varied leadership roles for students to shape the climate and conduct of the class. Here we can learn a lot from how out-of-school youth organizations position young people as partners in planning and decision-making.[5] In the classroom, this might look like a rotating responsibility to lead a check-in question at the beginning of each week and a reflective debrief at the end of the week, where students share what went well ("pluses") and what they'd like to change for next week ("deltas"). These are substantive roles, which contribute to shared responsibility for the classroom community and enable students to give feedback about course corrections. Although they may take some time to develop at the beginning of the year—through modeling and coaching to set clear expectations for roles that may be unfamiliar to students—this up-front work pays off. In a thriving classroom community, the teacher can let go of some of the work of managing the class and gain more inspiration from shared leadership.

We have seen amazing examples of this in our qualitative research, where teachers have created systems for sharing responsibility for the classroom, trusting their students, and ultimately experiencing joy in the process. In one classroom, two students served as facilitators for the meeting, but every student in the group had some sort of important role, such as leading research, communicating with public partners, or developing and leading icebreakers. The teacher described this structure with a building-block metaphor. Each role was key and essential to the project. Pulling out one block would cause the entire building to crumble. In survey research looking at student outcomes from TSV, these specific kinds of leadership roles were a major contributor to growth in student's sociopolitical efficacy and ultimately their engagement in civic action.[6]

Acts of vulnerability

In her influential book, *Subtractive Schooling,* Angela Valenzuela identified a pattern that continues to be a challenge in US schools: too often, high school teachers withhold their care until they feel that students have earned their trust.[7] Teachers expected students to care about their class before the teacher would show care for the student. The tragedy is that students may be unwilling to care about the material if the teacher does not care about them. It is a catch-22 that breeds mistrust and conflict.

Mistrust or distance can be overcome when teachers are willing to share something about themselves with their students. By *vulnerability,* we mean being open and honest about who you are, what you know (and don't know), and what you're feeling. Students are more likely to open up when the teacher is also willing to open up.[8] We have seen numerous examples of this in our own work. Maybe it's an example of a teacher being open about what they don't know about a topic, or their own uncertainty about broaching a particular subject with students. It could also be just a basic sharing of their story and how they got to be where they are. In one example, a female teacher shared that she was a feminist and preferred working with leaders who were women instead of men. This encouraged her students to share about their own values and preferences. We've also seen educators share about personal loss or failure in open ways that strengthened relationships and trust with students.

This vulnerability contributes to an ethic of care in the classroom. The teacher genuinely cares about the students and their well-being, and the students, in turn, develop genuine connections with the teacher. This often looks like teachers regularly checking in on the social and emotional temperature of their students. In some examples, we've seen teachers ask other students to check in on each other, sensing that a peer-to-peer connection may be more generative or healing than a teacher-student conversation. Similarly, we've seen teachers set up *ofrendas* (altars) in their classrooms where students and teachers could collectively share about loss and celebrate their loved ones.

Community rituals

Rituals do not get enough attention in research about teaching and learning. In referring to community rituals, we do not mean any old activity that gets repeated a lot over the course of a semester, such as the "ritual" of saying, "Okay, eyes on me!" For us, a community ritual represents a departure from the pace and stress of the day, to make visible a transition you want to make to the kinds of focus, reflection, and analysis that are needed for learning. Rituals signal, "We are a unique community." Learning how to participate in the ritual is a sign of membership in that community.

Eric DeMeulenaere, a professor of education at Clark University and former high school social studies teacher, described a series of rituals that his class used to set a tone for the day that centered trust, vulnerability, and open dialogue.[9] These involved small practices, such as starting the class in darkness with slides projected, to ongoing and iterative rituals, such as when they would "regularly gather around a makeshift altar to share personally about ourselves." In one unit, students developed their own booklets articulating goals and values, which eventually were placed on the altar for students in the class—and other classes—to view and appreciate. As DeMeulenaere writes:

> These rituals evoked a space and community associated with sacredness and emotion, rather than the traditional (and often alienating) intellectual space of school. They created a space for students and teachers to develop trust by connecting more deeply with each other's humanity.[10]

Rituals create a sacred space, in that they call for an intentional departure from unconscious habits or ways of interacting. Structured check-ins, or other intentional forms of interaction (reading circles, dialogue circles, reflective debriefs), are also rituals that deepen the humanizing practices of a classroom.

Group agreements and shared decision-making

Group agreements and shared decision-making are essential to classrooms where power is shared among teacher and students. Opportunities for input into decision-making—to be a participant in a school community whose ideas matter—are associated with greater belonging and connectedness.[11] Shared decision-making is facilitated by creating group agreements. By developing explicit group agreements and protocols for shared decision-making, the group is able to shift absolute authority from the teacher to a set of guidelines that all have agreed to. It's a very basic shift away from what moral development scholars call *heteronomy*, being ruled by others, to *autonomy*, being self-governed.[12] In prior research carried out by Ben, he observed a youth activist collective where group agreements became an important resource for dealing with problems that came up in the group, ranging from interpersonal conflicts to absenteeism.[13] These agreements shifted rule enforcement from adults' personal discretion to a resource that anyone could appeal to for guidance or mutual accountability. Youths' participation in shaping explicit ground rules, even if somewhat laborious, enabled them to be part of the process of how they wanted to learn together.[14]

Tier 2: Critical Conversations

After students and teachers have learned to share power, including be vulnerable with each other and manage disagreements, they should be ready to have critical conversations that bridge lived experiences with academic content through a lens of equity and justice. Here we use the word critical not as a synonym for negative, but instead reflecting its roots in critical social theory. Critical social theory is a philosophical tradition that calls for students to question appearances in everyday life and look for deeper truths or realities. It provides tools to expose injustices, disrupt dominant narratives that justify inequality, and question what we take for granted as normal or natural.

A contemporary example of critical social theory is Paulo Freire's idea of critical consciousness.[15] Critical consciousness involves the recognition that current features of the social order—and the intellectual frameworks that reinforce it—are not natural or inevitable but instead are socially produced. In the classroom, fostering critical consciousness means stepping back from the day-to-day to observe and discuss contradictions and tensions in everyday life. In Dane's class, for example, Jorge initiated a critical conversation when he commented on the contradiction between the college-going message of the school and its silence about barriers for undocumented students. Jorge's peers added their thoughts, and they were off and running.

Several studies have reported higher levels of academic engagement and learning for students who experience opportunities for critical consciousness in the classroom.[16] Students who have previously felt alienated or marginalized from conventional schooling begin to see how core academic practices can be a vehicle for personal identity and community uplift.

TANIA CAMPBELL, MIDDLE SCHOOL COUNSELOR (ON DIGGING INTO ROOT CAUSES)

 What I like about the program is that it gets the kids to think about what is real ... A big part of the program is to help kids identify the root cause, and that stops them and gets them to think about what really is happening and what is causing this and how is this related to, you know, what I'm feeling. And I, as a counselor, I think that's just a really great practice for individuals, but especially like when we're talking about making change in a building or in a community, really talk about those issues, like, get to the root of it ... You're not just worried about ... the symptoms, which you see and feel. I think that's a valuable thing, and even if the students don't get the resolution to a problem that they want, I think they learn so much from that, that they have learned to identify the root cause of something, and they don't always do that. I don't think most people are operating like that, and I think that's a step up for these kids. It's life-changing when you know how to do that. So I feel very strongly about that.

Critical conversations can also provoke reflective thinking about the social order of a school, which can then instigate a desire to push for change. Principals, like the one quoted in the sidebar, have reported how valuable this can be for addressing issues of exclusion and belonging. We worked with a teacher, Mike Walker, whose school's recent history included acts of xenophobia by Anglo white students toward Mexican American students. Students talked about an event the prior year when Mexican American students had shown up wearing the colors of the Mexican flag on Cinco de Mayo, only to face white students chanting anti-Mexican slogans, leading to fights and arrests. One student, Ernesto, noticed the double standard between St. Patrick's Day and Cinco de Mayo. After his friend said, "I don't like St. Patrick's Day because if you don't wear green you get pinched," Ernesto responded, "Yeah, and on Cinco de Mayo if you wear green you get put in the back of the police car." These students eventually worked on a project that promoted multicultural awareness across the school through assemblies and peer-to-peer teaching.

JEN PRITCHARD, HIGH SCHOOL PRINCIPAL
(ON THE POWER OF CRITICAL CONVERSATIONS)

 One student shared her experience of going into an all-honors class, which she'd been in her entire life, but then when it was less diverse, what that experience was and how she felt different and not worthy. And helping her see that the experiences she brought were different, not less. Just different...I definitely want to dig deeper into those kinds of conversations and have kids leading them so that they're learning from each other.

Sometimes insights about injustice have a spontaneous quality—they are not the result of a specific lesson taught by the teachers, but instead the result of creating a classroom culture that values student experience and risk-taking, where sharing power is the norm. But what might it look like to be intentional about bringing critical conversations into academic content teaching? We see this as a pathway to student engagement by anchoring academic learning in issues relevant to young people's everyday lives.

Critical conversations in the humanities
There are many excellent resources for exploring social issues in tandem with academic learning in literacy, social studies,

and civics. Literature teachers assign novels that surface conversations about racism, homophobia, and sexism. Skilled teachers weave opportunities for their teenage students to explore their own identities through the prism of novels. Social studies curricula, such as those developed by Facing History and Ourselves, offer a framework for students to study issues of power, conflict, and persecution in history and learn how to stand up to bigotry and hate in the present day.[17] Many critical conversations draw on the disciplinary practices of ethnic studies to help students learn more about themselves and their cultural roots. As quoted in an article by scholar Julio Cammarota, a student in Tucson's Social Justice Education Project described how powerful it was to learn more about the history of his family and community:

> Before this class [SJEP] I did not know who I was. I did not know where my family came from. I just was thinking about Christopher Columbus. And it just made me realize what everything is and who I am. You know, be proud. You know, be proud of who you are. It's the power—to know who you are and to be proud of who you are. It just, like, gives you power to do better for yourself—to keep learning, want to keep doing things. Because if you don't know who you are and you don't know what you are learning, you are like, "What the hell is going on?" You stay confused about life and about you.[18]

And there are wonderful civics resources, such as Street Law, that enable students to explore legal issues relevant to their everyday lives, such as interactions with school security and police.[19]

Critical conversations in math and science

In our experiences working with STEM teachers, holding critical conversations that bridge academic content to everyday life is far less common and faces more challenges. High school

STEM courses are accountable to specific content standards related to their subject matter. Moreover, some STEM teachers assume that math and science are "culture free," or meant to be explored outside of the messy world of conflict, power, and privilege. We encountered these barriers when teaching a class of in-service teachers seeking their master's degrees. Many of them were secondary science and math teachers, and they did not have permission or support in their schools to transform their whole curriculum. They wanted to be sure their students were learning the core knowledge of their classes, such as chemistry and physics.

The good news is, these teachers, demonstrating ingenuity and creativity, found ways to relate math or science learning to social issues that connected to students' lived experience. Consider, for example, the rich potential for students in a high school statistics class to master quantitative reasoning by exploring issues that affect them directly, such as disparities in access to health care, affordable housing, or healthy food. Several high-quality resources are available to support the high school math teacher in organizing a content-rich unit around publicly available data.[20]

Similarly, secondary science educators have been seeking ways to bridge science content with everyday life. The Next Generation Science Standards (NGSS), for example, focus on phenomena relevant to students' lives and communities, using driving questions that invite connections to students' everyday lives. As a leading NGSS curriculum development team wrote, "the combination of community science, technology, and a focus on science and engineering practices has been shown to help students feel more like scientists, including the belief that their ability to do science can make a difference in their world."[21] Daniel Morales-Doyle, a science educator at the University of Illinois Chicago, argues that STEM instruction needs to be anchored to social issues that matter to youth because of the ways this can elevate the funds of knowledge of students from marginalized communities and enable them to use science methods to transform their communities. Often these are topics related to the local environment, such as water, infrastructure, air quality, or urban heat islands. Such topics, investigated with the tools of chemistry, enable students to have conversations about injustice related to environmental racism or the differential effects of climate change.[22] To avoid leaving students with a negative or hopeless view of their situation, what Eve Tuck calls a "damage-centered perspective," Morales-Doyle and coauthor Alejandra Frausto recommend inviting a community organizer into the class and learning about the work people are doing to overcome these issues, so as to define the topic in ways that are "useful, hopeful, and locally determined."[23]

Summary

The examples above for humanities and STEM are meant to show how accessible it is to bring conversations about everyday life and issues that matter to young people into academic learning. This is not a new idea, but what is new is the effort to make it part of the culture of learning and inquiry across a school or district. We think of critical conversations as tier 2 of TSV in the classroom because it is an instructional practice that most, if not all, teachers in a school can do—with support. It is motivated by the well-established learning principle that students will be more engaged and motivated to learn when they feel a sense of belonging in the classroom and see the relevance of academic practices to their dreams and interests.[24] Developing a school culture in which teachers become skilled at facilitating critical conversations in an open and affirming way will advance the broader goals of Transformative Student Voice because of how it will contribute to academic engagement, critical consciousness, and belonging.

Critical conversations are valuable, but the true signature of a TSV school lies in creating structured and scaffolded approaches to youth-driven inquiry leading to research and action, which we discuss next.

Tier 3: Critical Civic Inquiry

Critical Civic Inquiry, or CCI, is a curriculum in which students complete a full inquiry and action cycle, starting with problem identification, moving to data collection and analysis, and culminating in policy proposals or dialogues with public audiences about their change agenda. In this, we owe a substantial debt to practitioners and scholars of Youth Participatory Action Research (YPAR).[25] In YPAR, learners draw on funds of knowledge, work together to address issues relevant to their lives, develop critical literacies, and claim meaningful roles in their schools and communities.[26] YPAR elevates the experiences of marginalized or minoritized young people and challenges deficit-based beliefs about young people.[27] One can find many examples of YPAR in out-of-school settings, such as community programs or youth organizing groups. It is less common to bring YPAR into the classroom in ways that hold on to its transformational aims *and* are paired with academic learning.

In our proposed tiered approach to TSV (as summarized in figure 5.1), a subset of classrooms and teachers would enact the CCI cycle. This cycle can be modified to suit varied lengths of time. In our experience working with teachers and schools, we recommend that the teacher give it at least one school quarter (about six to eight weeks) and ideally a whole academic year. The CCI cycle can occur in any academic content area—it is not intended just for civics class—so long as the subject matter can be learned through participatory action research. At the same time, we recommend that the CCI cycle be carried out in those subject matter classes that have the most alignment and adaptability to the demands of participatory action research, including being student-centered, relevant to everyday lives, and oriented toward action and change. For example, one model would be to introduce ninth graders to

CCI in their literacy classes, tenth graders in math (statistics) or science (biology), eleventh graders in social studies, and twelfth graders in civics. This approach exemplifies the notion of a spiral approach to curriculum in that it enables students to level up each year with greater challenge and complexity, while still experiencing repetition of core practices so as to achieve familiarity and mastery.[28]

There are several advantages to this spiral approach to the curriculum:

- Teachers from the same content areas can support each other with implementation and can develop tools and practical wisdom for engaging students over time.
- Students experience this kind of inquiry and action in different content areas, showing them how a variety of disciplines can be tools for problem-solving and community engagement.
- Teachers spiral their approach so that the expectations and rigor of projects gets progressively more challenging as students move through the grade levels.

This is, of course, not the only way to organize CCI at a whole-school level. We encourage school leaders to customize this based on your particular context, including teacher strengths and levels of buy-in.

ANTONIO GARCES, PRINCIPAL, SOUTHWEST HIGH SCHOOL

 I've really enjoyed the [CCI] experience. . . . Our kiddos have really engaged in a way that really . . . makes civics obsolete. I'm learning in this remote world how the content really drives the students' acquisition of knowledge. It's no longer simply saying, "You will learn history and get a B." It's more, what are you learning out of this process with regards to how to interact in society, particularly with issues, discussions, and government? So I am really excited whenever the kiddos take it on, especially the more challenging items.

Critical Civic Inquiry in the humanities

As of 2023, forty-one US states use the Common Core State Standards to inform their state standards for English Language Arts.[29] In contrast to previous standards that focused on students' ability to store, compartmentalize, and recall information, these newer standards stress complex reasoning, including argumentation, conceptual understanding, solving ill-defined problems, and applying information to new situations.[30] These strategies are well suited to open-ended inquiry in literacy. High school literacy classes typically include attention to the interpretation of texts, evidence-based reasoning about nonfiction texts, and writing persuasive arguments. Paulo Freire, after all, refined his theory of critical pedagogy while working on reading and writing with adults in rural Brazil. As his famous quote reminds us, "Reading the world always precedes reading the word, and reading the word implies continually reading the world."[31]

There is a growing field of empirical studies showing the impact of YPAR on literacy learning.[32] For example, one study described a project in which young people carried out original research about gentrification and showed improvement in key literacy practices such as writing across genres and public speaking.[33] In an example more connected to social studies, an eleventh-grade literacy teacher might adapt the approved unit, "Voices and Values: Growing Up Ethnic in America," by including a segment where students do research about the experiences of students from immigrant families in the school and communicate policy recommendations for the school or district that follow from their inquiry project. Looking back to Dane Stickney's yearlong focus on immigration issues that started this chapter, one can discern multiple literacy skills that students developed and practiced that year, including persuasive writing, textual analysis, and policy analysis.

In our experience working with USD, we have worked with many teachers who integrate the CCI cycle into their civics class. This approach is sometimes called *action civics* because of its focus on learning about civic rights and responsibilities, democratic processes, and levers for change through taking action. Core practices, such as critical reflection about experiences with racism or injustice, learning about issues that are relevant to one's life, and gaining skills to challenge injustice or discrimination, foster a sense of engagement and purpose in academic learning.[34] In our research, we have heard from students that the opportunity to engage in this combination of critique and collective action is rare. Students describe how these projects are bigger, more ambitious, and harder work. One student, Luz, distinguished between working on her CCI project, which had to do with rights for immigrant students at the school, and typical classroom projects:

> At first it was kind of boring . . . we started doing the project thing, and at first we were like, "Ugh, it's a project, we don't wanna do it. Ugh." And then we started getting into it, and we're like, "Oh, we're actually doing it," you know? "We're actually doing a big project, not just like a little class project." And it got better each day. [laughs]

Other students have highlighted the fun associated with doing original research. In this quote, a student at an arts school talks about their experience doing research about admissions processes at the school and how they could be more equitable:

> But it's definitely been, like, super interesting journey that, like, took us all the way back to our school's

founding and, like, those board documents from when the school was a brainchild. I found them and I nerded out over them big time, it was so much fun, with, like, my history teacher who gave me access. He was like, "This is so cool!" I was like, "This *is* so cool!" It was super fun, a lot of, like, good research and, like, data analysis that was super interesting.

We have seen all sorts of examples of topics that students want to take on. Some are focused on issues internal to the school, such as quality of school lunches, cleanliness and functionality of bathrooms, or access to AP courses. Others focus on neighborhood or city issues, such as food deserts or air quality. And in schools with high proportions of students from immigrant families, we have seen various types of action projects related to rights for undocumented students and tuition equity for in-state colleges.

Critical Civic Inquiry in STEM

Although it is more challenging in STEM, there are increasing numbers of examples that show how STEM teachers can move from critical conversations to critical civic inquiry. Daniel Morales-Doyle, whose work we mentioned earlier in the chapter, developed a youth participatory science framework where educators work alongside young people to identify problems of community interest, understand science and sociological contributors and potential solutions to these problems, and advocate for policy changes.[35] Megan Bang, a scholar of science education who incorporates Indigenous ways of learning and knowing, has worked with colleagues to develop tools to support intergenerational, decolonial, field-based science storylines in the Learning in Places Project.[36] Where requirements for standards alignment have been more strict, several curriculum developers have worked to build units that surface and anticipate student questions related to phenomena that are of cultural or societal significance and that challenge the idea that scientific and technical issues and solutions can be separated from social or political ones.[37]

Summary

TSV in the classroom requires a whole-school approach. We recommend a tiered system that identifies a baseline set of pedagogical practices expected of all teachers—what we call sharing power. In a TSV school, this would include strategies such as creating leadership roles for students, being vulnerable, enacting community rituals, and developing group agreements for decision-making.

Then, with a subset of teachers who demonstrate interest and capacity, we recommend an effort to bridge academic content with critical conversations about issues of justice and fairness in young people's lives. This takes humanizing practices further in terms of showing students how academic skills and knowledge, such as persuasive writing, statistical analysis, and historical understanding, can be leveraged to generate insights about the world around us.

The third tier of TSV in the classroom is to implement Critical Civic Inquiry as part of a unit (or several units) in a subject matter class. We recommend spiraling this process such that it rotates among subject areas for different grade levels. This CCI approach addresses standards for inquiry-based learning that call for students to formulate research questions, plan and carry out investigations, ground explanations in evidence, and be open to revising interpretations based on data.[38]

Each of these tiers will be a lift for most schools. Moving on them together calls for thoughtful, intentional, ongoing teacher learning and mutual support, which we discuss in chapter 6.

CURRICULUM AND PEDAGOGY CHALLENGES

Integrating and sustaining Transformative Student Voice in the classroom and the curriculum is a multistep process that will take several years. It requires engagement at many levels of the school and district. Our aim in this chapter has been to offer a framework for advancing this work in ways that are meaningful and feasible. Each of the three tiers we describe (sharing power, critical conversations, and CCI) have a strong base in research and many publicly available resources, including curriculum designed for specific content area standards. That's the good news.

At the same time, we are not aware of a school system that has combined these three tiers of curricular and instructional transformation in one whole school or district. It's a lot of change to manage and sustain. For that reason, we want to share some of the major challenges to anticipate and pitfalls to avoid.

Resistance

No surprise here. Not everyone will be on board with some of these changes. As we describe in the next chapter, we saw how a whole-school effort to foster student voice and critical conversations became fragmented because a subset of teachers in math and science did not see its value. They argued that such activities should only happen *after* students had mastered fundamental STEM content; they did not see how making connections to the lived experience of students' interests might be a *vehicle* for that mastery. We recommend that you and your colleagues who plan professional learning for teachers anticipate various forms of skepticism and take them seriously. Champions for this work from within content areas, particular science and math, will be key.

Resistance may also come, at least initially, from students. By the time they get to high school, many US students have become accustomed to certain ways of "doing school."[39] Listening to a teacher talk for forty-five minutes may not always be interesting, but it certainly asks less of students than engaging them in active learning. Students can grow attached to syllabi that are mapped out from week to week and assignments where there is one right answer. Such systems are easy to game—to learn how to check the right boxes. So when a teacher creates a more open-ended process, or invites students to decide together on an area of inquiry, or tells students the teacher does not have the answers, this might initially cause frustration. Teachers can prepare for this by making their decisions visible to students and inviting students to talk about their prior experiences with learning. This can open up space for students to look critically at their prior experiences of school and begin to notice that *schooling* is not the same thing as *learning*.

A second type of resistance from students may occur when talking about topics related to race, racism, and white supremacy. White students holding privileged identities, for example, may disengage or actively challenge the persistence of structural racism.[40] Students of color may not want to lean in to such conversations for a variety of reasons. In majority white spaces they may feel hypervisible, or they may be used to the unfair burden of being asked to explain racism or oppression to their white peers. Even in classrooms where students of color are the majority, they may question the teacher's motivations for introducing information about racial disparities or injustices, particularly if the teacher is white and their reasoning about *why* they are sharing data about disparities is unclear.

Deficit narratives are so ubiquitous in our schools that introducing conversations that explore disparities in achievement risk being taken as just reinforcing or reproducing those narratives. But it can be done. We offer guidance for how to explore issues of race, injustice, and inequity in our companion book, with examples focusing on how to approach them in an asset-based way with students, how to place the lens on gaps in opportunity (rather than outcomes), and how to leverage young people's everyday experiences and aspirations when selecting topics.

Ties to Academic Skills and Knowledge

The longstanding challenge in project-based learning, not just YPAR, has to do with balancing open-ended inquiry with the practice and mastery of foundational skills, such as writing, reading, and numeracy. There is ample research that, when done well, project-based learning leads to deeper learning and subject mastery.[41] But project-based learning is difficult to facilitate. Even the most experienced teachers may find it challenging to know the right amount of guidance to offer. Too little, and students spin their wheels or have trouble connecting their project to disciplinary knowledge. Too much, and students do not experience the agency and creativity that comes with open-ended inquiry.

Learning in small groups, which is a hallmark of project-based learning, has its own specific risks. What if there is one student in a group who really could benefit from focused support with writing, but that issue is disguised by the quality of the group report led by their peers? In our work to design a middle school, we addressed this by pairing long blocks of time for project-based learning with blocks of time designed for personalized coaching and support. For this work to serve students, it needs to ensure they are prepared for various kinds of communicative, quantitative, and other tasks they will face as they move through life, and we encourage you to design with this in mind.

Mismatch with Assessments of Learning

Most existing education systems were designed to assess narrowly defined content knowledge and skills. There is a deep mismatch between standardized achievement tests and the work products TSV students complete. Several years of our own systematic, mixed-methods research has documented growth in critical reflection abilities, political efficacy, engagement in sociopolitical action, and leadership skills.[42] One of our team members, Beatriz Salazar, has documented the powerful role of learning from failure and setbacks that students experience in these projects.[43] Yet none of these outcomes are part of existing assessment systems for students. These outcomes matter, but they don't translate into student assets that are visible to schools, colleges, or future employers. Education systems miss out on students' varied expressions of ingenuity, criticality, persistence, and civic agency.

A second, related problem with this mismatch is that we don't have ways of giving feedback about what *quality* looks like. Not all YPAR projects are the same. Teams make mistakes; their research methods may be poorly executed; student presenters may not have thought through who their audience is. These issues, such as research design, persuasive policy arguments, and intrateam accountability, all distinguish lower- from higher-quality projects. Formative assessments that enable teachers to share feedback and students to assess themselves are essential for student learning and quality projects. Assessment systems that are attuned to the ups and downs of experiential, open-ended learning can ensure that students and teachers give and share feedback along the way that contributes to everyone's learning.

CONCLUSION: IT'S WORTH IT!

This work challenges business as usual in US schools; you will be leading change work at multiple levels of your school system. And it is worth it. The reasons to adopt TSV in curriculum and teaching are too compelling not to try.

Students will feel more connected to their teachers and will see the relevance of what they are learning. Being part of CCI projects will equip them with critical skills for democratic participation and civic engagement. This may be the first time they are exercising agency over their learning and taking on key leadership roles for their classroom learning community. Marginalized students, in particular, may experience feelings of belonging and dignity that have been painfully absent from their educational journeys. Opportunities to communicate their social change ideas with audiences of school leaders may provoke anxiety, but it is a healthy kind of stress—the kind that precedes learning and empowerment.

Teachers, too, benefit. The initial call to become a teacher—to be there for students, to contribute to a young person's growing consciousness of the world, to share your excitement for the possibilities of academic knowledge—these all get reinvigorated in a TSV approach. The job of teaching becomes less about preparing students for tests or managing behavior, and more about accompanying students on an unpredictable journey of empowerment and insight. Most importantly, if your school and district can green-light this work, your teachers will experience the reward of being in community with other teachers as they do it. No more lone wolves.

If you're a principal, a district administrator, or a curriculum lead, you won't be facilitating these projects, but you have a key role to play as listener, question-asker, critical friend, and advocate. It's fun to meet with students. We encourage you to stop by classrooms doing this work to ask how it is going and see what questions students have. Invite students to organize more formal check-ins where you can give preliminary feedback on their project ideas. Give feedback, but don't squash ideas, even the most audacious.

SIX

Afterschool Clubs, Summer Sessions, and Professional Development

AFTERSCHOOL AND SUMMER SESSIONS can be an amazing opportunity to start, extend, or supplement your Transformative Student Voice work, but if it's not happening throughout the school day and year, it's probably not enough. Summer sessions offer an opportunity to do some intensive work with young people, but the scope of what they can do is limited by the time period, and often by a lack of access to other students and school personnel whom they might want to include as subjects of their research activity. These sessions require a bit more planning and focus, but they can be a great way to introduce young people to the process or to focus in on a very specific collaborative project. Even better, a summer session can be used to set aside time for a group that has been working together during the school year to really dig deeper and get a project finished up. As an afterschool program, you can engage young people year-round, they have more access to other students and educators for data purposes, and you can avoid some of the challenges associated with a class—students can be part of the program all the years they are in the school, so you build in longevity and the opportunity to keep new students coming in. You also avoid the challenge of accountability to state tests and content standards when integrating the work into content classes. It's important to consider that afterschool clubs often attract students who have already bought in to the structure of schools and won't draw those students who just want to get out of school—and the latter students have a lot to say about what needs to improve. The biggest challenges with afterschool programs are connected to logistics. There are competing activities (sports, arts, other clubs) and often challenges related to transportation or, for older students, work schedules. A few schools we work with have used their expanded lunch periods or homerooms as a place for clubs that include student voice work, which can alleviate some of the challenges of afterschool scheduling. In the next section, we'll explore some of the programs we've seen, then discuss strategies to make this option a part of your range of opportunities for Transformative Student Voice. Finally, we will take the opportunity to share insights on how professional development supports all of the student voice efforts—if you mean to do this work, you must provide quality, ongoing supports to the educators who will work with students. We'll share the key elements of effective professional development for adults, and also discuss how students can be effective facilitators of some of this professional learning.

CASE STUDIES

With a University Partner

Western University served as a site for the GirlsInTech program, a summer camp funded by the National Science Foundation, with a focus on exposing Black and Brown girls to technology careers. The program has girls identify a problem they'd like to solve in their community, research that topic, and then use a range of technology applications to raise awareness of the issue and its solutions. They use simulation programs, podcasting, game creation, app development, iMovie, and other technologies both in the research and in building solutions. This type of programming can fit into a portfolio of student voice offerings, not for its technology focus, but because of the focus on identifying a problem, researching it, and then proposing solutions. The technology is an important element, but the transformative part is the conversations about inequity and the focus on getting to solutions to challenges through research.

EBONY, STUDENT PARTICIPANT

 Because of GirlsInTech, I have really grown out of my shell and can present with a lot more confidence.

Programs like this have multiple advantages. They provide summer learning opportunities for students, they build specific skills, they include research projects that contribute to our understanding of the issues at hand, and they are funded. These programs may be located on university campuses, or they may be offered in your district, if you can provide space. Often they are specifically designed to engage more marginalized students, and in turn benefit the district's need to provide additional support and opportunity for voice for those students. The caveat? All money is not good money, and all student programming does not equal student voice.

If you are interested in building this kind of opportunity for your students, start by developing relationships with local universities. Reach out to the deans of the appropriate schools or colleges. Education is often a good starting place for research that supports young people and their voices, but STEM, the arts, and social sciences often have potential as well. The dean should know their faculty and be able to make connections between you and faculty who are working on areas of interest to you. A program may already be designed or in place, such as the GirlsInTech program or the Rural Schools Climate Project we discussed in chapter 3, which is an example of a district working with a university faculty member to design a project and seek grant funding. In fact, most of our work in TSV and CCI over the past fifteen years has been grant-funded, with the university researchers seeking funds and partnering with local districts on programming.

In recent years, research-practice partnerships (RPP) have become a popular way for school districts to partner with university researchers.[1] The main advantage of RPPs is that they leverage research to improve practice. In contrast to traditional models, where researchers come into your schools and study a topic of interest *to them*, in this model, research questions and project aims are coconstructed among researchers and practitioners. When working as they should, these are spaces where district staff and school leaders can shape a research agenda to be useful to your work. For example, our TSV research team is currently working on a codesigned project with students and teachers from USD. As we presented in chapter 4, the district has a thriving program that supports student voice and leadership, but it lacks assessments that document the kinds of learning and growth that young people experience. They asked us if we would facilitate an effort to codesign a student leadership assessment with teachers and students. This benefits the district, because it will create practically relevant, useful, feasible tools that the program can use to document student learning. It also benefits us and the broader education field, because we will publish articles describing how to codesign in this way and develop tools that we can then share in other educational settings. RPPs like this are a terrific way to bring in university partners on the grounds of shared decision-making and practical research. In the process of developing such partnerships, it's important to identify the goals you want to meet—and if Transformative Student Voice is part of your agenda, then conversations about how you'll meet the elements of that work will be critical at the design, implementation, and evaluation stages.

SEAN OVERTON, SCHOOL SUPERINTENDENT (ON STUDENT VOICE)

 I think that our teams have really demonstrated to teachers that our students can step up and take the lead. I think it's . . . demonstrated [to] teachers that they don't always need to be . . . the ones who are taking the lead on issues of importance, and we don't always need to be the ones who are . . . above the students in terms of the hierarchy; that we can all learn from each other.

On Your Own

Designing and developing your own afterschool or summer programming is more work but also brings more reward. Start by pulling together a group of teachers and students to imagine the possibilities and identify the challenges. One of the first challenges likely to be named is funding—after all, educators who work summers need to be compensated, and other costs (for program materials, meals, transportation, and supplies) will be incurred. Talk with your business office, or whoever in your district is responsible for grant funds—all districts receive federal funds to supplement state and local funding (Title funds), and many of the Title funds can be used to support programming for students. A quick summary of the possibilities:

- Title I is about "improving the academic achievement of disadvantaged students," and we have shown that student achievement can increase as a result of participation in TSV and CCI programming.[2]
- Title II funds are to be used to provide supplemental activities that "strengthen the quality and effectiveness of teachers, principals, and other school leaders," and we've shared examples in previous chapters about how young people worked with educators to develop (and deliver) professional development for teachers.[3]
- Title III supports English language learners and developing and implementing language instruction educational programs—a summer program using a CCI and TSV approach, with an additional focus on language acquisition, seems like an easy win.[4]
- Title IV is about supporting safe and healthy school environments, providing a well-rounded education, and supporting the effective use of technology. Climate work fits, but so would arts and technology programming.[5]

Really, any set of funds could potentially be used if you approach it with the question in mind: *How could these funds be used to include students or support TSV efforts?*

ANN HARRIS, SUPERINTENDENT, SOUTH COUNTRY SCHOOL DISTRICT

 We have a really active student voice club. The middle school student voice club last year was a very important part of shouting out to us that we had to change our code of conduct, and they were very instrumental in changing our dress code; that really came about from them at the end of last year. And then this year, we put in place when we were developing—we got this from Deerfield Middle School—they had a wellness room, so we knew we wanted a wellness room that we could not have afforded to fund if it wasn't for the grant. And because we knew that our kids now more than ever need breaks, they need a place to just have a break. Because going all day in the classroom is a long struggle. None of us go all day long without a break. So we wanted to create a student break center, and the student voice club was instrumental every step of the way in developing and producing it and designing it, and so we just rolled it down, it took us almost half a year to roll it out. This was our student voice and our student voice moderators. They rolled out this Student Break Center, instead of calling [it] a Wellness Center.

In another example, several districts designed a summer program over the course of four years using funding from a US Department of Education school climate grant that was part of a research-practice partnership (the Rural Schools Climate Project). Students spent three weeks working on various projects connected to the goals of the school climate grant. In one school, students and teachers worked together on the design of a sensory pathway for their elementary school; in another, they identified the in-school suspension process as ineffective and problematic—and not aligned with the stated goal of the school to be using trauma-informed and restorative practices—and so they created a Student Break Center (see figure 6.1). They designed the room to have comfortable, quiet space, created norms for using the space, and made a video to roll out the idea to their peers. The school hired a coordinator to staff the room, and they collect data on usage through check in-check out forms. The students meet regularly with adults on the climate team to review the data and tweak the process. One notable change—the room was working as a quiet, reflective

FIGURE 6.1   Student Break Center goals

Student Break Center Goals

The new Wellness Room will have the following goals, which align with the four pillars of the equity grant:

1. Promote **social and emotional well-being** for all students that address a variety of student needs.

2. Create a **calm and safe space** for students to take a break from some of the typical stressors of school life.

3. Set up students with strategies or skills to **return to class to accomplish what needs to be done.**

4. **Prevent** students from exhibiting negative behaviors when they are feeling frustrated, overwhelmed, etc.

5. Provide a **quiet space** for students to make up work if they were absent or are behind for any reason.

6. Establish and build **positive relationships** with staff and peers.

space, but some students also needed an energizing space, so conversations about how to incorporate both are in progress.

Another group identified the dress code as unfair and biased against girls, and that group spent their summer sessions updating the dress code to be more inclusive and gender neutral, developed guidelines for teachers to be more consistent and familiar with the process for addressing dress code issues, and prepared procedures to better communicate the dress code to students, families, and staff.

There are likely a range of other funds available that you could use. In one city in the West, we hosted a summer Migrant Youth Leadership Institute each year, supported by funding from the state's education department. This was a weeklong residential program for migrant students in which they did arts-based activities along with student voice projects connected to migrant education. Consider federal, state, and local funds, along with local nonprofits and foundations. Partnering with local organizations, such as the Salvation Army, Boys and Girls Clubs, or your local parks and rec department are all avenues for exploration.

Within Existing Programs

You probably already have numerous clubs and afterschool programs in your schools, with passionate educators running them, and students already engaged. What if you took the approach of deepening the TSV elements of those programs? In South Country School District, the middle school had two very active afterschool clubs—Girls LEAD and PRIDE. The Girls LEAD club is about empowering girls to achieve personal and professional goals, while the PRIDE club is about providing a safe and supportive space around topics of gender and sexuality. Both had core elements in their existing programs that aligned with student voice work, primarily a focus on developing agency and power connected to identities. Neither, however, had a commitment to doing research or working to change systems—but both were excited about the option once they were made aware of it. In fact, it was members of these two clubs who participated in the summer camp mentioned above that resulted in creating a more gender-neutral dress code.

BROOK JONES, ASSISTANT PRINCIPAL, SOUTH COUNTRY SCHOOL DISTRICT

I did the student voice summer camp the past two summers. I'm involved in more of, like, a negative perception type of process with investigations, so to go and be a part of something where I watch these brilliant young minds be able to speak their mind and see it—it's been a great opportunity for me to be a part of something, but also a great opportunity for our kids. And in our student voice meeting last year, we had a student speak up and just said, "you know, one of the issues that we have is there's not female hygiene dispensers. So, if I have an issue I can't go to the bathroom and get the supplies that I need." She spoke up, we call operations, and they fixed it. Because she spoke up, you know, so we're like, "sweetheart, you don't need to make that your project. We can fix that right now." And the change is being made by the students and I'd like to continue to see that, you know, because we're in a very different world than you and I went to school. It's very different.

Similarly, Oak Knoll High School had a robust social justice club and Summit High had a multicultural club—both with the goal of raising awareness around issues that students were concerned about. Both were already doing good work around developing critical consciousness and identifying issues, but both needed to extend the impact of that work by having structures in place to help them look at root causes, collect data, map power, build alliances, and develop policy recommendations.

MALCOLM WITTE, PRINCIPAL, URBAN ARTS ACADEMY

We started with a club. It was done after school. It was something that, I believe, Terry was interested in driving it. And Terry has been at my school for the better part of six, seven years. So he was interested in it. He became engaged with it, and then it moved from an afterschool club to a midday, like a lunch group. So I kind of said, "Hey, if you're going to run this lunch group, I'll get you out of lunch duty. Run with it." I saw the development of kids into leaders. I saw the development of kids with regards to their voice and the development of kids with regards to their presentation skills. And those three things, I'll tell you, they're—we call them soft skills sometimes. And I'm like, "That's a shame.

Those are as hard skills as humans need with regards to the next step in the postsecondary world—education, workforce, whatever you're going into."

If considering aligning with existing programs, it's important to do a good job of aligning goals and of preparing adult facilitators or teachers. Revisit the questions we posed in chapter 2 when forming your teams—make sure the teachers who run those programs are onboard, have a shared vision of what adding TSV to their club will look like, and provide them with professional development and resources to make the shift.

SUMMER PROGRAMS, HOMEROOMS, OR AFTERSCHOOL CLUBS? OR ALL THREE!

As you think about how you want to design opportunities for students to participate, you'll want to look at the existing afterschool and summer programs in your community and identify any organizations who do youth development work. You can provide space and access to students, and they have staff and experience running summer programs. As you consider the options, assess how good a fit each might be for integrating tenets of TSV work—how do the goals of the club or program align with ideas of empowerment, agency, and change? Keep in mind that this isn't about service learning or workforce development—it's about civic engagement, empowerment, and youth leadership. Think about who the teachers are who currently support those clubs or programs, and what support they will need to transition toward a TSV approach. Do you want to create your own TSV-specific program? If so, where will the funds come from? What teachers might be recruited to lead? How will you find time to provide training for them?

Think back to chapter 3, where we talked about the importance of including young people on existing teams—climate teams, curriculum teams, equity councils—do any of those meet in the summer, such as for a retreat? Or would some of the members of those teams be interested in leading a summer program for students to engage with the goals of the team and incorporate TSV into their work? Or could you just use funds from the various Title and other grants to develop a summer program specifically focused on TSV? Each of these choices has advantages and challenges. We'll explore the challenges next.

Challenges

Funding

If you are running the program yourself, you'll need funds for teacher stipends (for training and for the sessions), supplies and materials, snacks or meals, and transportation. If you are working with a youth organization partner, they may have funds for staff and sometimes stipends for youth, which is a good incentive for participation, as it reduces the competition of summer jobs.

Transportation

If you are planning an afterschool program, how will students who take the bus make it home? Reliance on families to transport might limit participation for students who really need to be included and heard from. If it's a summer program, same problem. How will students, especially those whose parents are unable to transport them, get to and from the program? Some programs we have worked with have provided students with monthly passes to access public transportation in order to facilitate their participation.

Scheduling

In all of our afterschool programs, we have scheduling conflicts—for both students and adults. Students sign up in the fall but then play a spring sport, or teachers commit to the afterschool club, but they also coach. As students get older, they may have work or family care obligations. These can be barriers to participation for all or part of the year. In the summer, for middle school and early high school students, the summer program can be a great option and meet some needs that families have to provide a safe and structured summer activity—but as students get older, it can conflict with summer employment.

Time constraints

The constraints of time and participation in summer and afterschool programs can create a sense of urgency, on the part of the adults, to get something done—and that can mean the voices and participation of young people are minimized. Or, because of time constraints, adults enter with a problem already in mind, so young people are really supporting adult goals rather than coming to their own ideas. The time crunch, especially in summer, can also limit the opportunity to collect robust data, which then weakens the arguments young people might make for policy change.

PROFESSIONAL LEARNING AND SUPPORT FOR TEACHERS

Upon reviewing the CCI curriculum, one social studies teacher, Raymond, summed up his thoughts succinctly: "This is really cool, but you're asking *a lot* from teachers here." He's not wrong; doing this work can feel unfamiliar, uncomfortable, and even scary for educators. But, we argue, it's doable and worth the work.

Having said that, to advance this work responsibly, school and district leaders need to provide consistent, abundant, high-quality support for teacher learning and reflection. As an administrator, *do not pass go* if you have not created a plan, in partnership with trusted teachers, about how your faculty will be engaged in professional learning related to each of the three tiers of sharing power, critical conversations, and Critical Civic Inquiry.

As your team begins to plan for this professional development, we recommend that you organize supports around two types of learning. The first, what we're calling *transformative adult learning*, speaks to the mindset shifts toward vulnerability, self-reflection, and empathy that this teaching approach requires. The second, what we refer to as *project management skills*, focuses more on the distinctive types of pedagogy that tend not to be emphasized in teacher education programs and are unusual in US high schools. We describe each next.

Transformational Adult Learning

Teachers must first engage in personal work. When thinking about sharing power with students, educators must consider their role in fostering agency and a sense of belonging in the classroom. We outlined some of the specific practices that contribute to a humanizing classroom in chapter 5. In this section, we encourage you to design supports for professional learning that are themselves transformative.

Shared community purpose

Transformational learning is best pursued in a community of peers, with time to develop and deepen trust and shared purpose. Engaging in activism work with youth can be emotionally, psychologically, and physically draining.[6] We've often watched one or two really skilled and dedicated teachers be asked (or forced) to shoulder the bulk of grade-level or school-wide justice issues. This can be isolating for those teachers; we've heard them label themselves *lone wolves*. This is too much to expect. Some kind of community of learners is essential.

There are many ways to structure this kind of community of shared purpose. A few years ago, we offered a graduate course in which in-service teachers enacted the CCI curriculum in math, science, and literacy classrooms. They met regularly, debriefing readings, planning curriculum, and seeking one another's input and advice. As Shelley and colleagues wrote, "They could bounce ideas off one another, commiserate when they struggled, and celebrate when they succeeded. This brought the lone wolves into a pack, and there is power in the pack."[7]

This trusting, honest, and supportive environment could also take place as part of professional learning sponsored by a school or district. Whole-school professional development can pose its own challenges. Teachers often have different degrees of openness to talking about race, class, and identity, all of which tend to pop up when teachers engage in CCI with students. That can make it difficult to achieve the shared purpose we mentioned earlier. In one instance, in partnership with Joe King, the principal at Vista High School, we attempted to teach the CCI approach to all the teachers in one high school. The math and science teachers refused to engage in the sessions, saying that while math and science could potentially address issues of injustice, the students lacked the needed skills. Instead, these teachers argued, they needed to walk students through the acquisition of basic skills before they could be used to examine social issues. At the same time, a group of social studies and English teachers quickly broke off from the group, eager to put the new learnings into play. With such a fragmented and unaligned group of educators, the professional development series did not achieve the goal of schoolwide CCI—and it left us frustrated.

Creative spaces for experimentation

We have had more success in bringing teachers together from different contexts to achieve that shared purpose and even achieve something harder: a creative space. One professional development unit served social studies teachers from across the district who wanted to teach the CCI approach. They quickly aligned on the importance of the work. At the end of the first session, they started riffing: sharing tips, tricks, lesson plans, and other resources with each other. More veteran teachers would model minilessons or provide think-alouds through tricky topics. Newer teachers would seek advice and even practice an introduction to a rigorous task or deeply think through a discussion protocol. Everyone wanted to know how they could rebalance their curriculum to have less of the usual stuff and more student activism. In this space, the group sidestepped squabbles about *what* they were doing or *why* it mattered; instead they could support each other in deepening their ability to facilitate such a demanding curriculum. Teachers from that curriculum regularly attended happy hours and backyard barbecues with each other, and the core group continues to informally share curriculum and other resources with each other.

Emotional and political support

This work is out of the ordinary, often not supported by administrators, and can be emotionally taxing. The current political landscape in many states and districts makes it risky: diversity, equity, and inclusion programs in schools and universities are being dismantled in many states.[8] While we reject efforts to dismantle or cease DEI initiatives in schools, we have observed uneven quality in how it is approached in professional development. Some of it (like the offerings from Learning for Justice) is outstanding.[9] But we've seen materials and been in trainings that are of poor quality. Sometimes they are overly didactic and essentialist in their treatment of identity categories; other times facilitators do not ask enough of participants and allow some teachers to remain on the sidelines without engaging. In other words, just because a training focuses on justice doesn't mean it's a quality training. We're setting a tall task here: trainings must build shared purpose, allow for trust and experimentation, and enable teachers to stand strong together as they take on challenging topics. This means considering the political and social backlash that teachers may face for conducting research around a topic and proposing a policy solution. That is *political* work, and that's risky in today's climate. Even CCI projects that are not partisan by definition, such as demanding free menstruation products in school bathrooms, or calling for truthful teaching of US history, could create a minefield for educators depending on the context. As such, professional development offerings must be solidarity spaces, with teachers providing emotional and even political support for each other as their students lead them toward potentially tricky problems being addressed in possibly risky spaces. In other words, a support system is needed to keep these invaluable educators in the game of supporting student-driven research and policy creation.

Student-led professional development

We have seen several schools where student teams designed and led professional development for teachers. Topics have included culturally responsive teaching, student-teacher relationships, and student-centered curriculum. One of the most impactful elements of student-led professional development is that through the very act of participating, conventional power relations between students and teachers can be transformed. Students are positioned as the experts and bring that expertise to the facilitation of the session. Ben attended a student-led professional development for teachers. The student facilitators opened with a check-in question: who do you think has it harder these days, students or teachers? The students asked us first to reflect, then we went around the room to share our thoughts. This opened up a space where teachers shared some of their challenges while also giving voice to concerns they had for students. The student facilitators held the discussion and used it as a jumping-off point to share instructional methods that increase student engagement.

At Southwest High School, students implemented professional development that received positive feedback from attending teachers. But the students expressed frustration: most of the teachers who were attending were already pretty good at culturally responsive teaching. They felt like they were preaching to the choir. They asked us for help in how to get the more reluctant or nonengaged teachers to attend. They argued that if the teachers who *should* be there *would* be there, then student-led workshops would be far more impactful. This issue of voluntary versus mandatory participation is a challenging one. We recommend starting small, and if that means attracting teachers who are already supportive, that's a good place to start. Once you and the students are confident in the quality of their trainings, including evidence from feedback, then they could challenge the first cohort of teachers to each invite one colleague to participate in the next sessions.

Project Management Skills

While engaged in transformational learning, educators should also start considering nuts-and-bolts strategies that will benefit them in facilitating TSV in the classroom. Unlike the typical classroom, where pace, assignments, readings, and lessons are set in advance by teachers, conducting action research with youth is different. It is more emergent. The adult is more a partner than a leader. The research process may require significantly revising a topic or choosing a new direction altogether. This requires the teacher to be nimble, supporting students on the new, emergent path. It might also call for teachers who are comfortable with a lack of control and even the possibility of failure.

Professional development for this kind of role needs to focus on skills that, more likely than not, teachers did not encounter in their teacher education classes. We are thinking of skills that range from how to run a good meeting, to how to delegate tasks, to how to create systems for small group accountability. We think of these skills as technical because they are less about gaining insight into identity or issues of power and privilege, and more about how to lead and manage projects in ways that scaffold student engagement and success.

For teachers adopting the full CCI curriculum, one of the key shifts that we have found helpful is to see their role as more of a project manager. Because students are engaged in emergent just-in-time learning, the teacher becomes more accountable for facilitating a rigorous *process* than for delivery of specific kinds of *knowledge*. We have worked with teachers, for example, who are expert in supporting multiple teams of students who are working on distinct elements of a class project. Such teachers have drawn on common practices for agile project management in the software industry, such as the scrum method, which offers many tools for small-group accountability, long-term planning, and diffuse tasks.

DEREK WHITE, HIGH SCHOOL TEACHER (ON FACILITATION)

 It was interesting, because right off the bat, you know, I've . . . never written a student Bill of Rights. I, we, had no template, but that was kind of the design, I told them right off the bat, "My goal here is to help you stay organized . . . or to open these meetings. I'll send . . . recap emails, and I could be the note taker, but this is your process." And so student leaders stepped up right away, and just led it, so I didn't have really much to do with the creation of bill, other than some light editing. Occasionally I'd throw out some ideas, but you know they really completely led that, that entire process, and I was just, you know, keeping them hyped up, creating breakout rooms, keeping them motivated, that was really all I did.

Many of these skills are best learned through modeling and coaching. Do your school leaders run good faculty meetings? Faculty meetings can be a context to be reflective and intentional about the features of productive, engaging, and affectively satisfying meetings. Similarly, faculty meetings can offer short, fifteen-minute mini workshops on a range of skills that can help teachers support students with carrying out complex projects on difficult topics.

CONCLUSION

Afterschool and summer programs absolutely add value to your efforts to increase opportunities for student voice, and they can have the added benefit of leading to university and community partnerships. They provide an opportunity to be creative, to engage students who may not be as connected to the standard offerings of school, and to engage students outside of the structural constraints of the academic year. Perhaps most importantly, these programs can be the quickest and easiest way to start up your student voice work—get that easy win in at the beginning.

This chapter also wraps up our section on implementation—we shared the story of a district-level program, then explored how a curricular approach works, and wrapped up with the discussion of afterschool and summer options. Then we laid out the key elements to consider and include in the professional development you provide for the educators who will work with young people in these Transformative Student Voice opportunities. If you return to chapter 3, where we shared the levels of TSV—advise, collaborate, lead—you can map the various approaches we used in this section to that framework and begin to see what you are doing well, how you can expand, and where you are missing an opportunity to include young people in your school transformation work. Most importantly, we hope that this section on implementation has shown you how Transformative Student Voice connects at the district and school level, classroom level, and extracurricular level.

SECTION THREE

Bringing It All Together

IN THIS FINAL SECTION, we explore what happens when student *voice* shifts into student *activism*, that is, forms of expression that challenge district policies and practices from the outside or through more confrontational tactics, and then we try to bring it all together.

If districts and schools don't attend to student voices, grassroots organizations and community activists almost certainly will. These organizations often end up as adversaries to districts, because, when unheard, young people use media and public spectacle to express their ideas, which can be embarrassing to district leaders and make collaboration challenging. School districts, for their part, too often exclude activists from decision-making tables and fail to deliver on promises. It does not have to be this way.

We argue in this chapter that districts are missing out on the energy and vision of key stakeholders when they do not make an effort to develop relationships with grassroots youth activist groups. And they have much to gain through more creative, solutions-oriented partnerships. We communicate this through multiple examples. In one example, we observe how tensions emerged between community leaders and district leaders that led to acrimony and conflict. We use this primarily as an object lesson in mistakes to avoid. Another example chronicles the development of a lauded partnership between Poder Comunitario, an intergenerational organizing group representing marginalized communities, and Urban School District. The partnership focused on reducing disparities in referrals to police, with the broader vision of ending the school-to-prison pipeline for Black and Brown youth. Using field notes, interviews, and public records, we show the time commitment it took to build trusting relationships, the way the meetings were structured to invite and support youth participation, and the accomplishments of the group in creating a first-of-its-kind memorandum between the district and police. Overall, this chapter draws on examples to illustrate the benefits that follow when district leaders proactively build relationships and engage community organizations in complex change processes. Community activists can act as resources whose perspectives and people power accelerate equity-based reform. The chapter offers a playbook for engaging the district's most vocal critics as partners in decision-making and implementation.

Our final chapter brings together the key ideas we have explored throughout the preceding chapters. We explore the benefits of TSV for districts, schools, educators, and students. We address challenges you might face in implementing TSV and how you might overcome those barriers. We then reinforce strategies that, regardless of setting, are crucial to the success of TSV. Finally, we end with considerations for assessment, including how to create authentic assessments and cultivate existing data.

SEVEN

When Voice Becomes Activism

PICTURE IT: you're caught off guard when you hear that a local youth organizing group is holding a press conference on the steps of district headquarters calling attention to racist treatment by school police. Or you show up to a school board meeting and encounter dozens of youth and adult community members using the public comment period to demand more bilingual and bicultural school counselors.

Outside pressure brought by activists can be a headache for district staff and leaders. Community groups are often the most outspoken critics of district policy. They sometimes use tactics that maximize media scrutiny, such as school walkouts or press conferences on the steps of district buildings. You may not always feel that they acknowledge the long-term, behind-the-scenes efforts your district staff are making to reduce inequities and improve outcomes. Activists will sometimes use whatever legal means necessary to criticize, cajole, and instigate.

But youth activists are also, most of the time, right. If you're reading this book, you probably resonate with the values of progressive, social justice–based activists who call for our education institutions to be more inclusive, equitable, and anti-racist. Since at least the 1960s, high school student activists have played essential roles in pushing schools to be more culturally responsive, anti-racist, and inclusive.[1] The 1968 Chicano Blowouts in Los Angeles, for example, drew attention to inadequate education for Chicane and Mexican American students. Student activists in the 2010s challenged the overpolicing of students of color and persuaded school boards in multiple US cities to shift toward more developmental and restorative discipline practices.[2] The increased adoption of ethnic studies courses in the past ten years grew out of explicit demands from youth of color to have their schooling support and be accountable to the needs of the urban communities.[3] Youth groups supporting rights for LGBTQIA+ youth have fought successfully for the establishment of gender and sexuality alliances across the US.[4]

So we have an impasse. On one hand, progressive youth activists and districts are often adversaries in public spaces. On the other hand, the two camps share similar end goals. The differences may stem more from political pressures, institutional constraints, and forms of accountability than from different values or visions for the future. We think these different contexts can be bridged through creative partnerships that prioritize shared aims. District priorities will be strengthened when the energy and insight of activists are part of your coalition.[5] How do you want to engage with students when their desire for change steps outside the lines of student voice and leans into activism? What might it look like for you, as district leaders and staff, to engage grassroots activists as partners in the work of building better schools? Our purpose in this chapter is to share several examples from our prior work to provoke reflection and discussion about where things go wrong and how they can go right.

REACTIVE APPROACHES TO STUDENT ACTIVISM

Over the years, we've partnered with many kinds of groups seeking to advance education justice, including outsiders, such as community activists, and insiders, such as district leaders or classroom teachers. Unfortunately, it feels like it's been the norm that outsiders and insiders have not worked together, even if they share substantial common ground. There are many reasons for this: There might not be available channels for activists to share grievances. Activists may have reached out to district leaders without getting a response. Or they might have gotten a response, but due to legal and human resources privacy requirements, the district was unable to share all the information, leading to frustration. Or, they got a response, but it was contrary to what they wanted. These varied reasons can lead community members and students to adopt classic activist strategies. And this means that districts are often caught flatfooted and in a reactive mode, rather than being ready to proactively engage. Here we highlight a few cases where this occurred after activists used outside channels, such as social media and walkouts, to get their voices heard.

Social Media Firestorms

Social media is ubiquitous in our everyday lives. We use it to connect, to share updates, and to see what others are up to. It's no surprise, then, that social media has become a popular tool for activists and organizers. Activist movements for human rights in Egypt, educational access in South Africa, and racial justice in the United States have all made effective use of social media to organize ordinary people, broadcast political platforms, and challenge tyrannical authority.[6] Social media is not the villain. It's a vehicle for expression. Looking at when students resort to using it is instructive, and it may be an indicator that there are no other channels through which they can get their voices heard.

At Tri-City Regional School District, four vice principals are in charge of discipline—one for each grade level. A few years ago, a few white and Black students in the sophomore and junior classes got into a fight, with discipline results that included in-school suspension for the white students and out-of-school suspension for the Black students. The day that the Black students returned from suspension, they informed the principal that they were going to stage a walkout. The principal followed protocol: they notified the district office and school staff, informed students of the consequences of missing class and leaving school property, and tried to ensure the safety of the students who chose to participate in the walkout. What they did not anticipate were the posters that students created and carried during the walkout, which named two of the vice principals, included their photos, and included racist statements that students said those vice principals had made. These images hit social media, were shared widely in the community, and resulted in both VPs receiving a barrage of hateful responses and messages. The teachers, VPs, and other school staff felt that the district and school should have protected them, and they filed union and HR complaints. Because of the HR and union grievances, further actions remained confidential, and students, educators, and the larger community were unaware of the consequences or outcomes, which left many people unsatisfied.

In another example of social media use, in a different district, an outspoken group of students used social media to express solidarity with their teachers, who were in contract negotiations with their district.[7] They called for sit-ins and teach-ins and other expressions of solidarity with their teachers across the district. When posting a video titled "Support Our Teachers," they included the phrase "blow up the district"—referring to getting students to inundate the district with pro-teacher messages (as in, *blow up their phones*). The video went viral and resulted in hostile, racist backlash online. Some observers took the phrase out of context and considered it a violent threat against district staff. To help manage the situation, a key adult mentor of the student speakers brokered a meeting with the district superintendent to clarify the intent of the message and promote dialogue. No disciplinary action was taken against the students.

From the standpoint of your legal or public relations teams, these two examples might be seen as headaches that soak up time and energy. They might recommend some sort of disciplinary action against the students. The potential for harmful consequences of social media posting are real. But we encourage district leaders to take seriously the values and impulse driving both actions by students. For students at Tri-City Regional, their posts were a response to what they viewed as racist, unfair, differential treatment of Black students. Although we don't know all the details of the incident, it resembles a pattern that has been well-documented in research about differential, harsher treatment for Black boys in schools.[8] In the second example, the students were trying to find ways to support their teachers. One of the students who posted the video later said that their activism was sparked by one of their favorite teachers, who had to leave the school because of their inability to afford local housing on a teacher's salary. Wouldn't we want students to care for, and stand with, their teachers?

An Unsanctioned Walkout

Racist comments and taunts made by a small group of white students had been an issue for Black students at Oak Knoll High School for most of the fall semester, and the students had discussed their concerns with the school principal and some teachers. The district and school leadership had used its harassment, intimidation, and bullying (HIB) process, but they judged most incidents as unfounded. When, eventually, they did find an incident to meet the HIB criteria, the consequences for the offending students were not shared publicly.

By spring, students were fed up. They felt like the school was doing nothing to address the problem and that there had been no consequences given to the perpetrators. In addition, the Black students felt like they were given harsher disciplinary consequences than white students. These two grievances motivated students to partner with a community organizer from a neighboring county for support with strategy and raising public awareness. To draw attention to their concerns, the students staged a walkout three days in a row at lunch time, drawing media from the surrounding cities and states.

If you were in a leadership role at the school or district, what would you do in response to student walkouts that were not supported or sanctioned by school leadership? Should the students be disciplined? Do you ignore the issue and hope it goes away?

In this case, the superintendent saw that the existing protocols available to address racist comments and taunts by students were not adequate. District leadership had the wisdom to see that there were deeper issues going on and that treating this as merely an issue of bullying had not addressed those issues. The superintendent met with students and promised to engage a task force, provide training for faculty and staff, and support the creation of a Transformative Student Voice group in the school to identify issues, research them, and pose solutions. As of this writing, the task force is meeting regularly, a first round of training for all staff has happened, and the TSV group will begin work this summer.

A School Board Meeting Takeover

"We do not recognize your authority!" shouted the executive director of City Students United (CSU) at the members of the Metropolitan School District board. The board members left the room and called security, while students and organizers from CSU and members of Educators 4 Change held a "People's School Board Meeting," which was captured by waiting film crews. The issue? A school attended by CSU students would soon be adding metal detectors at the entry to their building—the result of a policy shift at the district level from allowing schools to make their own decisions about metal detectors to mandating that all schools use them.

The students in the CSU chapter at that school were opposed to metal detectors. Their focus for the year had been on increasing counselors, not cops. In chapter meetings, the students researched information on the impact of metal detectors in schools as well as district policy. They wrote letters to the administration and school board. They scheduled themselves to speak at the board meeting, and they organized a demonstration with posters and signs prior to the meeting. After speaking at the board meeting, the CSU students and allies from multiple community organizations watched as the board went to vote, and it became obvious that the mandate would pass. As they saw this happening, the CSU executive director and the students took over the meeting, stating they would not recognize the board's authority and calling an end to the meeting while occupying the meeting chambers. All of this was captured on video by local media outlets and shared widely on news channels and via social media. It was an impressive show of solidarity between CSU and allied groups, but ultimately, the vote went through to implement the metal detector policy. And, shortly after, the principal disbanded the school chapter of CSU.

Putting aside your opinions about the metal detector policy, the outcome is unfortunate. With CSU no longer allowed on school grounds, current and future students would no longer have access to this civic leadership opportunity. CSU is a community-based organization, founded by students to demand a high-quality education in their public schools. Its model has students forming partnerships with teacher sponsors, who create a chapter of CSU in the school so that students have a space to meet before or after school. School-level chapters work to address issues specific to their own schools, and students can also participate in the citywide chapter, taking on districtwide concerns. Banning CSU from a specific school sends a message that only some kinds of political protest or activism are acceptable.

What went wrong here? And how might it have been handled differently? In the next section we share the story of a more proactive approach to engaging community and youth organizers.

A PROACTIVE APPROACH WITH YOUTH ORGANIZERS

Like many big-city districts, in the 1990s USD began putting more police officers in schools and using police to respond to everyday behavior problems. The passage of zero tolerance rules meant that even nonviolent infractions could lead to tickets, suspensions, and sometimes expulsion. The Annie E. Casey Foundation reports that there was a 72 percent increase in "secure detention" from 1985 to 1995, even though less than one-third of the youth in custody had been charged with violent acts. Students, disproportionately Black and Brown, were getting sent to the police for offenses that in past eras would have been handled by school personnel.[9] This phenomenon came to be called the school-to-prison pipeline, because of the ways in which school discipline not only mirrored the carceral system but also left students with records that tracked them into adulthood.[10] Getting suspended or expelled is correlated with lower education outcomes and a higher likelihood of jail in adulthood.[11]

By the 2000s, the local consequences of these policies became evident to students and families in USD. Poder Comunitario (PC) became involved in the issue when they began to see their membership, which was mostly Latine, Mexican American, or Chicane families, face increased criminalization in schools. PC had a long and proud history of organizing parents and students to identify problems in their schools, gather data through participatory approaches, and use the data to catalyze change. PC used a combination of insider and outsider strategies: sometimes they worked collaboratively, such as when they worked with district leaders to bring new school models to their city, but other times they adopted pressure tactics that brought public awareness to injustices or inequities in the district.

To sharpen their work to disrupt the school-to-prison pipeline, PC collaborated with a national civil rights organization and community organizers in two other cities to study, document, and draw attention to disparities in school discipline in USD. Imagine you are a school or district leader who learns about this collaboration and the report. What might you do?

What Would You Do?

A local community organizing group is preparing to publicize a report documenting a problem in your district. It could be lack of access to AP courses by students of color; it could be racial disparities in suspensions and expulsions for the same offenses; it could be about the failure to recruit and retain teachers of color.

- Do you call your legal team to get them to quash the report?

- Do you remain quiet and hope the whole issue blows over when the news cycle passes?

- Do you call the organization's leaders to explore how to work together to address the problem?

What happened next is unusual and exciting: USD and PC decided to partner to address the problem. And this was not just a one-off display for the cameras. They developed a partnership with dedicated staff, spanning several years, which started with the development of a new disciplinary code and continued with efforts to monitor implementation and stay accountable to the aims of the code.

Partnering with activists around compliance and implementation is new terrain for district-community partnerships, and it entails some risk for districts. It means inviting activist groups behind the scenes to see data as it is gathered in real time. It means letting them know where the weak spots are with implementation. It takes trust that community partners won't take advantage of the situation to expose or embarrass you. This risk, however, is worth it.

The Power of Student Lived Experience

JACK BRONSEN, ADMINISTRATOR, USD

 For me to hear a student say, "Here's how I've experienced this in my own school. I was thrown in handcuffs," or, "I was dragged out of my school and thrown in the back of a squad car because I got in an argument with my principal over what I had in my hair that day," or things like that—I mean, the narrative is powerful because it's completely contrary to anything you would want a young person to experience and what our system in theory should be designed to fight against.

This partnership was successful in bringing students into the process of monitoring the new reforms. A core group of youth leaders from PC, made up of current high school students and recent high school graduates, learned the policy details and data analysis skills. Youth leaders, along with adult staff, participated in ongoing meetings with district officials to monitor the progress of the policy. Students reviewed the data about disciplinary referrals, raised concerns about inconsistencies in implementation, and put officials on the record about their plans: *What is USD's plan to eliminate racial disparities? What schools have restorative justice?*

These regular meetings were punctuated by a yearly accountability meeting with the superintendent and district staff, in which PC issued a report card to the district and proposed specific actions that the district ought to take. While the regular meetings tended to focus on internal discussion and negotiation, the accountability meeting was geared toward the public and aimed at highlighting accomplishments and failures of the district. These accountability meetings were not praise fests. At one of the meetings we attended, student leaders gave out grades for different elements of the data and then asked the superintendent for comment. PC assigned one B+ but also Ds and Fs, with the worst marks going to the continued problem of racial disparities in referrals to law enforcement.

Why would the district commit resources to this partnership? As the quotation from one of the key district players suggests (in the sidebar), it was mutually beneficial. It lent credibility to the district's efforts and heightened the visibility and urgency of addressing the problem. Working with young people in the monitoring process, in particular, enabled the district to learn from the youths' lived experience, including those most harmed by carceral discipline practices.

JACK BRONSEN, ADMINISTRATOR, USD

 It was very much a mutually beneficial partnership because the leadership of the system was eager to make change in this space. And sometimes you need not only your own voices as system leaders but external partners . . . that have political . . . presence in the community elevating things to demand attention to them. So that's a great example of research that was done, both quantitative but also fieldwork that was qualitative around the student experience and the educator experience that brought to light some things that needed significant change in the system and that . . . resulted in pretty radical policy shifts.

Positive results of this partnership included the district hiring and training dedicated restorative justice staff at almost half of the district's schools.[12] As the work continued, the local teacher union joined the coalition, which strengthened its mandate. According to the district, there was a reduction in overall suspensions. At the same time, the problem of disparities in referrals to police did not go away, debates about how the district should handle school safety persist, and the restorative justice practitioners need ongoing training and support. But we highlight the work of this partnership, and particularly the role of students in it, as a bright spot worth emulating.

PRACTICAL LESSONS

The examples above show different paths that youth activism can take and varied ways that districts and schools responded. You can try to shut activists out or limit their influence, but this is unfair to students and, we believe, will be self-defeating for school and district efforts at equity-centered reform. Here we offer ways to approach community youth activist groups that can ultimately lead to partnerships that strengthen your work.

Find Common Ground

Not all activists will agree with your values or policies. We have seen in the past decade a rise of right-wing activism that counters decades of progress in making schools more inclusive, respectful, and fair. Moms for Liberty, for example, uses activist tactics to pressure school boards to eliminate rights for trans and LGBTQIA+ students. A range of conservative groups are pressuring state and local education boards to teach a white supremacist version of the past that grossly misrepresents US history. Although we have not seen examples where *students* are part of these campaigns, it could happen. More to the point, there may be community groups that espouse positions that are flat out wrong or that you simply don't agree with. In cases like these, we suggest differentiating between local people and national organizations.

In our experience, local groups, including highly conservative ones, have a stake in the school district. For example, in chapter 3 we shared the story of Noble Township's equity council and how it created space for authentic student voice at the district level. That equity council, which advised the district on equity-related issues, was intentionally made up of diverse representatives—students, staff, teachers, administrators, and community members. And those community members included several who represented very conservative interests. It took time and intentional training to build the capacity of the group to engage effectively across differences, but with local people, it's possible. In that group, for example, the conservative members generally opposed adding LGBTQIA+ topics into the curriculum. But through a process of sharing stories and hearing from all sides, they were able to lean in to the idea that no child should ever be made fun of or bullied for their beliefs or practices, and that while they were free to teach their children their own beliefs at home, the school could not pretend that LGBTQIA+ students and families don't exist—and so they need to make space for those families as much as they make space for conservative Christian families. The tension remains, and the balance of how to address issues that arise is revisited often, but communication is happening, and the trend is toward finding common ground that is inclusive and affirming for students.

National organizations without local membership, on the other hand, are often more focused on performative displays. In that case, partnering is not an option; it may be time to bring in your best communications people and figure out a public relations strategy to counter negative attacks.

What we want to speak to in the remainder of this chapter, however, is a different situation: one where progressive or justice-oriented youth activist groups are trying to influence district policy. Don't be dissuaded by the tactics these groups use, even if they embarrass you or hold your feet to the fire. These are just tactics. See if you can find common ground around end goals. If you see common ground, it is worth moving to create a coalition that makes those shared commitments explicit.

Build Trust and Create Internal Agreements

In our experience with community-district partnerships, it is common for each party to think they are the weaker or more vulnerable side. District leaders are afraid of the negative attention they could get if the community partner were to criticize them. Community organizations see a far better resourced district, with its leadership's ties to the political elite of the city, and they fear being shut out of decision-making, or worse, losing their access to local philanthropy.

Ben saw this play out in a partnership he was part of, which was studying a high school closure in a large urban district.[13] A small grassroots youth organizing group asked Ben for assistance in studying the impact of school closure on displaced students through a participatory action research process. To study that impact, they needed access to district records and permission to recruit students. They needed a sponsor from the district who was willing to work with a youth group that had been vociferous in its criticism of the district, including leading school walkouts and identifying the roots of its decision in structural racism.

At the first meeting to discuss a possible agreement—among district staff, the youth group, and Ben—everyone's different assumptions about power and voice became clear. The district representative, a white man, expressed his fears about the power of the group to embarrass the district. He was afraid that the group might use access to the data to claim a gotcha moment and release it to local news. He wanted assurances that this research project would not be biased or predetermine results.

The community organizer, who was Black, had a very different take on the meeting. He pointed out how the district administrator, while describing his group as a powerful critic of the district, assumed power in the meeting by controlling the agenda, asking all the questions, and ending the meeting unilaterally. The community organizer said that he was treated like a "peon" in the meeting.

We encourage you, as a district leader, to see the kinds of asymmetries of power that may exist between you and grassroots youth activists. Yes, you may be concerned about their ability to bring in news organizations or criticize you, but more often than not, the district wields a kind of power that vastly outweighs small community organizations. Your funding is stable, you enjoy access to local political officials, and your salary is probably far more than what the community organizer is being paid. The life cycle of districts typically outlasts those of grassroots groups.

In a context such as this, building trust is paramount. Group agreements can help. Ben remembers in the school closure study everyone agreed to a few simple elements: There would be no surprises, meaning no releases of findings before everyone had had a chance to discuss them. There would also be a commitment to open-minded review of the data, including results that might conflict with what the youth expected or the district partners wanted. And we would check in regularly. We didn't promise to become friends; we didn't need to agree about everything. But these simple ground rules enabled us to work productively together for the ensuing year.

JACK BRONSEN, ADMINISTRATOR, USD

 And then we would also negotiate where we thought things were headed and ensure that—part of the importance of these types of partnerships—you've got to have some guiding principles around no surprises in some cases. We have to agree that we're opening things up to everybody, and we need to be able to have conversations about those before they go public, or live, or things like that.

Monitor Implementation Together

In two of the examples we shared earlier, Oak Knoll and USD, the district leadership saw value in developing a coalition of stakeholders who would develop action steps and monitor implementation together. What stands out is the way that these coalitions included a range of actors, including students and representatives of community organizations from outside the district. These kinds of coalitions are of great value for monitoring how a new initiative is unfolding or being carried out. As Bronson said above about the school discipline partnership, students have the potential to share aspects of lived experience that can inspire action and also hold everyone accountable for staying committed to reforms. In other research, Shepherd Zeldin, an expert on youth-adult partnerships, has found that nonprofit organizations stay truer to their missions when young people are part of governance.[14]

What is key, however, is that such partnerships are attentive to the differences in power and privilege among adults and youth. In such cases, guidelines for youth-adult partnerships are valuable. Our team developed a set of dos and don'ts with two student partners that offer a good start, as shown in figure 7.1.

FIGURE 7.1   **Do's and don'ts for adults in youth-adult partnerships**

Do...	Don't...
Listen for understanding when talking to students about their experiences.	Step in with assumptions that you know what youth want or don't want.
Understand that young people are like adults—we also want to learn and grow.	Talk more than the youth partners.
Be vulnerable.	Be condescending or talk down to students.
Be ready and willing to learn from young people.	Say, "That's not possible."
See youth as experts in the conversation.	Take things personally.
Share power and resources with young people.	Use youth for your own aims.

Note: Draft created by transformative student voice team of youth and adults (2022).

A big part of any effort to monitor implementation is to develop routines for looking at data together. USD and PC did an excellent job of this by bringing in the district's research office and also seeking out partnerships with university researchers. This kind of opportunity sends the signal that decisions will be driven by how a new program or policy is actually working (or not). It also is an opportunity for students to learn and practice how to use evidence to make decisions and develop policy. Last but not least, it's another space where you are building the capacity of your adult staff to partner with young people in respectful, equitable, and productive ways.

CONCLUSION

Grassroots community organizations fighting for equity and justice often end up as adversaries of school districts. When trust is lacking, youth activists use media and public spectacle to embarrass district leaders and make unilateral demands.

School districts, for their part, exclude activists from decision-making tables and fail to deliver on promises. It does not have to be this way.

In our view, saturating your schools and districts with multiple and diverse opportunities for students to share their perspectives and participate in policymaking is the right approach. A TSV district would have strategies that get at all three levels of voice spelled out in chapter 1: students as leaders, as collaborators, and as advisors. But even the best-designed, most comprehensive approach will face shortcomings. Things will happen that you can't plan for. Some processes for managing student grievances just won't be adequate. Also, if you're lucky, there will be community organizations and student unions that are also interested in the welfare of your students and have advocacy agendas they want to push. In these cases, student activists will step outside the lines; student *voice* will turn into *activism*.

We recommend a proactive approach to student activism that emphasizes empathy, deep listening, and solidarity.[15] In the reactive approaches that we've shared in this chapter, you can see how problems escalated in ways that provoked hostility and polarization. In contrast, proactive approaches focus on root causes rather than symptoms; they try to get at *why* students are frustrated or angry and take that seriously. The proactive approach invites community groups and activists in to formulate alternatives and monitor progress. Districts miss out on the energy and vision of key stakeholders if they do not develop relationships with grassroots youth activist groups. And they have much to gain through more creative, solutions-oriented partnerships.

EIGHT

Conclusion

ONE OF THE BEST THINGS about being an educator is when your students find you, years later, and tell you about the impact you had on them. Perhaps it is a student telling you how you inspired them, how you cultivated a love of learning a certain subject, or how your words encouraged them and helped them through a difficult time. While we might get glimpses of our students' growth over the years, the truth is, we never know, in the moment, the lasting impact we are having. But we do know that if we are intentional about creating spaces to share power, to listen, and to learn from young people, that we do impact them, in the moment and for a lifetime.

The Lasting Impact of TSV

Jorge didn't remember the words "Critical Civic Inquiry" or "Transformative Student Voice" after working through our curriculum as a middle schooler. But he certainly remembered and came to embody the act of surfacing a problem, working in community to better understand it, and acting to ultimately address the issue. As a sixth grader, Jorge called out his charter middle school's college themes as hypocritical and offensive when nearly 40 percent of the students were undocumented, which posed serious barriers to attending college. Through a TSV project, Jorge and his classmates lobbied legislators to allow undocumented students access to in-state tuition and established a scholarship for undocumented students. But that's not what stuck with him. The excitement of researching a problem and learning more about his own Latine roots was sparked in the TSV project, but it endured for years. Jorge, who originally thought he wouldn't go to college, not only attended a state university but was active in a multicultural fraternity, doing justice-oriented community service. Years later, Jorge said that moment of being heard in class, naming a problem in the school, was major. But even more important, he said, was the *process* he learned to address things that are unfair in life. He described power in naming the problem, discussing it with others, conducting interviews to learn more about the problem, and finally, work-shopping creative solutions that could be implemented. While it sounds simple, Jorge said, the process has been powerful in his life and educational career. He isn't alone. One of his other class-mates served as the campaign manager for a successful bid by a progressive city council candidate. Another said she channeled the care found in TSV into being a nurse. Still another continued to hone her understanding of social inequities and became an immigration lawyer. While all of these youth did amazing things on that student voice project, it's been fun and deeply rewarding to see how the TSV spirit continues to live and grow in them in different ways.

The story shared above, while reflective of one student's experience, is not an isolated incident. Many of the teachers we have worked with over the years share stories of youth returning to thank them for how classroom experiences of voice and agency impacted their lives. We have also received thanks from students who have gone into careers in politics, teaching, and community organizing who describe being inspired by their experiences engaging in critical reflection, research, and activism as students.

Something special happens for young people when they elevate their voices and take steps to positively impact their schools: school becomes more relevant, they find a community in their student voice team, some find healing in addressing social injustices, and they realize how they possess the power to shape social systems.

Similarly, we have also seen classrooms, teachers, and schools change for the better through student voice and activism. Classrooms become spaces of lively discussion and engagement. Teachers see students through a new light and learn to be more culturally responsive. School-level changes, although less obvious, have also occurred, such as smarter teacher hiring practices, more relevant classes for students, student-centered approaches to bullying prevention, and restorative approaches to school discipline.

This all leads us to ask, why wouldn't every school leader and educator want this experience for their students?

In this concluding chapter we want to reinforce the key takeaways of this book. We also want to provide one last set of reminders of some challenges and how you might overcome them. We highlight those practices that, regardless of setting, contribute most to positive outcomes. Lastly, we will give some considerations for assessing TSV impact.

KEY TAKEAWAYS

As we approached this text, we, the authors, considered what we wanted you, the reader, to walk away with. Clearly, we wanted to share with you the benefits of TSV, but we wanted to be balanced, and let you know that it would not all be sunshine and roses, and share how you might overcome some of these struggles. We return, for a moment, to chapter 1, where we introduced the idea of visionary pragmatism, a theory developed by Patricia Hill Collins, which reminds us to keep our eyes on the ultimate vision, even as we make pragmatic decisions along the way.[1] It matters to have a clear vision and a strategy for checking in with yourself and your team, in order to make sure that the choices you are making move you closer to that vision, even when the daily challenges of time, resources, bureaucracy, and resistance to change get in the way.

Benefits

Throughout the first seven chapters of this book, we have extolled the benefits of youth engagement in TSV. In chapter 1, we highlighted some of our research findings that document the impact of TSV for youth participants. Here we want to focus on the benefits of TSV for schools, educators, *and* students. To that end, we will discuss the unique youth insights that come from TSV, increased engagement of TSV participants in school, and the potential for expanded critical consciousness of students.

Unique insights

In all our talk about the positive impacts of TSV on youth, we often neglect to address how TSV programs positively impact districts, schools, and educators. The clearest benefit of a TSV program is the unique insight that youth can provide. In chapters 3 and 4, we described how youth can contribute to school policy and practice. Recall the story we told you of youth giving Ben and Carlos a tour and highlighting blind spots in the school video camera system. Also, we addressed how youth sharing their experience with adults in an equity committee led to increased understanding of the experience of young people. In both of these cases the insights possessed by youth could be used to improve the policies and practices of schools, thus making schools safer physically and psychologically for students. The depth of understanding that is possible in collaborative encounters like these far exceeds anything that would be possible in a simple survey of youth perspectives.

We also want to reiterate that TSV programs have the potential to highlight the insights and experience of students from marginalized communities—particularly in the realm of diversity, equity, and inclusion. In chapter 3, we shared a student presentation in which youth described how teachers responded to incidents of bias and discrimination. In chapter 4, we gave the example of the information system that students of color developed to identify educational allies and warn each other about adults to be avoided. Through TSV, youth have an avenue to share their lived experiences with adults who might not ordinarily be privy to such perspectives. However, the sharing of youth stories is not sufficient. To truly capitalize on this knowledge, school leaders must leverage this information to develop or revise school policies and practices, ideally with the participation of students and teachers.

Increased youth engagement

Carlos was recently invited to present at a national conference for elected officials on the topic of youth engagement in schools. A few attendees lamented what they saw as a lack of responsibility in youth; they saw young people as being more interested in social media and being influencers than in doing well in school and engaging with their community. Carlos challenged this thinking by noting the limited opportunities youth have to contribute to their schools and communities. TSV addresses this void and encourages the engagement of young people.

Through involvement in TSV, youth have access to a group of motivated peers and a caring adult. We have seen how older students mentor younger students through the action research process—helping them to eventually take leadership roles. These points of contact give students a reason to engage with schools.

In chapter 5, we also mentioned how TSV groups became a space for affirmation and relevance for students. Affirming students and their identities is a powerful tool for engagement, particularly for students from marginalized backgrounds, who do not regularly see their culture and heritage represented in school curriculum. Similarly, TSV provides educational relevance for students as they investigate issues that directly impact their lives and, along the way, learn academic and civic skills.

Engaged students care about their schools. They take steps to make their schools better places. Additionally, engaged students perform better in school. The combination of these things will improve school climate and potentially impact school ratings.

Critical consciousness

In an age where school outcomes are dominated by standardized test scores, the importance of critical consciousness has been neglected. Critical consciousness allows young people to question the validity of an argument, to look for what might be informing someone's perspectives, and to make connections in information that is not seemingly linked. These skills are crucial for postsecondary success, whether in college, the job market, or civic life. They are also particularly important in an age of artificial intelligence, disinformation, and political division.

Though it can be a challenge to assess critical consciousness, through chapters 3–7 we provided examples of how youth engaged in TSV demonstrated critical consciousness and used that consciousness to impact their schools and communities. In chapter 5, and again at the start of this chapter, we shared the story of Jorge, who questioned his middle school's emphasis on college-going. Jorge's critical consciousness inspired research and persuasive letter writing to state politicians to provide in-state tuition rates to undocumented students, helping lower the barriers he and his classmates faced in accessing higher education. In chapter 6, we shared about various afterschool and summer programs that use elements of TSV and promote critical consciousness in youth. Improving critical thinking and consciousness can only be positive, as it will likely aid in postsecondary success, help students to be a more critical consumers of media, and inspire civic engagement.

Activism seems to be a bad word in some segments of the country and with certain political groups, but the reality is that youth activism has inspired social change throughout US history. In our work we have seen former TSV participants become climate activists, advocates for voting rights, and political staffers. These youth describe how the critical consciousness they acquired through their student voice experience inspired them to want to make a change in their communities. These young people left TSV experiences feeling powerful and wanting to make an impact on the world.

Challenges

No matter what setting you ultimately choose for implementation of TSV, you will almost certainly face challenges. By anticipating challenge, you can be better prepared to respond and ensure the success of your TSV program. Here we want to highlight three common challenges TSV programs face, regardless of setting: ensuring participation, meeting resistance from stakeholders, and implementing large-scale programming.

Ensuring participation

As a school leader, you might have school policies that limit youth participation in school leadership or extracurricular activities. Additionally, you might come across colleagues who believe that only high-achieving students deserve a voice in schools. In either case, limiting participation in TSV will hamper your ability to leverage its benefits.

The most common limit to participation in TSV has to do with requirements placed on students, often based on grades and disciplinary record. As we addressed in chapter 4, limiting participation to high-achieving students robs schools of the insights of those for whom school is *not* currently working. Also, as we addressed earlier in this chapter, TSV programs provide a pathway for engagement in schools. To highlight this point, here is an example from a TSV school partner.

Engaging "Problem" Students

Over the fall semester, the student voice team at Cook High School became increasingly frustrated with their school principal. The team had asked multiple times for a meeting with the principal and for access to school data on student discipline, but were not given either. Through a state education website, the team found some data that showed a disparity in disciplinary action between white students and students of color, but they were hoping for more current data—and to talk through their concerns. As the semester was ending, members of the team took to social media to express their frustrations. In their posts they criticized the school leader for being nonresponsive and asked for her to resign.

When the student voice team returned for the spring semester, something odd happened. They found that most of the team had their class schedules changed, and they were no longer enrolled in the leadership class that housed their student voice program. What is more, those who remained in the course found that the new students in the class were students who typically had disciplinary problems and lower grades in school—what many might consider "problem" students. The student voice participants felt this was an act of retaliation on the part of the principal.

The remaining team members updated the new students on their voice project, its goals, and the data they had collected thus far. This is where things got interesting: the new students became engaged; they shared stories of the seemingly minor infractions that led to suspensions and of feeling targeted by the school administration. These students had insights and experiences that provided more robust data to the team. Additionally, the new students were motivated to gather more data from friends who also had disciplinary records, to help with the data analysis, and to help shape disciplinary policy.

Without these new team members, the student voice team from Cook would not have had the insights of students who experience disciplinary issues. What we think is more important, though, is how these students who were considered "problems" began to show engagement in school. Our argument is this: students need an opportunity to contribute and be a part of a team—even those students that might currently struggle in school. Rather than excluding those students from TSV, involve them and watch how their interest in school increases when they are learning about issues relevant to their lives.

In addition to limits related to academic performance, it is also wise to consider how access to student voice might be limited based on a program's setting. In chapter 6, we address how afterschool and summer TSV programs might limit the participation of students who play sports, work, or require transportation. Here it becomes important to be creative. Can students be provided a stipend for their summer participation, lessening their need to work, or provided with a bus pass? Either of these ideas make TSV more accessible to students.

Perhaps the most detrimental limit to TSV is when authentic student voice is not incorporated. When adults have predetermined agendas, or when groups are not facilitated well, the potential of student voice is lost—TSV becomes an academic exercise, or one merely put on for public perception. Other threats include symbolic voice, where students hold no actual power, and interest alignment, when student voice is only promoted if it aligns with the interests of adult leaders. For student voice work to thrive and achieve its fullest possibilities, students must be in the driver's seat and have an opportunity to inform policy. Later in this chapter we will address practices that are essential to making TSV thrive.

Encountering resistance

When you implement your TSV program, be prepared to encounter resistance. In chapter 5, we discussed how some teachers might be resistant to implementing TSV. This might be because teachers feel their subject area does not align with TSV or because the practices of TSV do not align with their teaching skills and training. Some students might also be resistant, since they have become accustomed to working in a more prescriptive schooling environment. These students struggle to break out of a lecture-based teaching style to one that requires them to actively engage in learning and practice critical thinking skills. We have also addressed how some school leaders might be resistant to TSV and the practice of sharing power with students. In all of these cases it becomes important to stay the course and engage in dialogue with your colleagues to help them understand the benefits of student voice in schools. As teachers, students, and school leaders see the positive change in students, they will likely become enamored with TSV and its positive outcomes.

Resistance from adults is almost certain to occur when student voice groups begin to aggressively criticize school policy and practices. In chapter 4, we gave you some ideas for how to prepare yourself and respond to student critique. Though you or your leadership team might not like being the target of students, remember—as we noted in chapter 7—students are usually on the right side of history. Additionally, take pride in the fact that you are an educator in a school where students are confident in using their voices to advocate for their needs.

Implementing at scale

In multiple chapters we have noted that it is hard to implement student voice at a larger scale. Even in the district approach we described in chapter 4 it was challenging to get implementation across all schools. Sometimes this is because of the adult commitments that are required for implementation. We spoke to this in chapter 5, describing how some teachers, compelled to attend a TSV training, were more hesitant. Leadership changes can also disrupt existing agreements and force a renegotiation or recommitment to TSV work. Though imperfect in many ways, the relational approach to scaling we previously described is one way to bring on teachers and school leaders who have values more aligned with student voice. However, we would argue that when a district makes student voice central to its mission, then it can use these values to identify and train teacher candidates who will implement TSV authentically.

WHAT MAKES TSV WORK

Throughout this volume we have provided you with insights on how to implement TSV in ways that make sense for your school or your district. In each chapter we shared tips and examples from schools or community settings. Here we want to highlight themes that are key to making TSV work regardless of setting. We will also narrow our gaze to things that you as an adult leader can do to support the success of your students. To that end, we want to address TSV leadership, adult training, support systems, youth-adult partnerships, and community partnerships.

TSV Leadership

A strong leader for your TSV program can make all the difference in the world. As we described in chapter 4, your TSV leader will help to navigate tensions between youth and adults. We also demonstrated, in chapter 6, how a good leader finds funding possibilities for TSV by being creative with budget and grant opportunities. It is hard to say if there is a specific skill set that makes for the perfect TSV leader, but a leader who can navigate school politics is helpful. We would also add that a good leader, even if they are not involved in day-to-day student programming, must be able to develop and nurture relationships with students.

Adult Training

Despite their best intentions or desire to support student voice, adults will need training on how to implement TSV. For most, this starts with a shift in mindset. In our companion volume, *Transformative Student Voice for Teachers: A Guide to Classroom Action*, we start with addressing the assumptions and beliefs we carry as educators.[2] We also provide guiding questions for educators to ask themselves prior to starting student voice work. In chapter 3 of this book, we described principles of an equity training that were useful for adults to be more receptive to engaging with youth and hearing their voice. We reiterate that all educators should engage in some self-awareness work; even teachers who lead or sponsor student clubs—where the assumption is these groups are more student-centered—should always be asking how to make their spaces more student-led.

There are also technical skills to learn in how to guide a student voice project. We have said this before, but no teacher education or school leadership training program will give you the specific skills required to be a good TSV facilitator. Again, we refer you to our companion volume for specific direction on facilitation practices, but we want to highlight important ideas here. As an adult leading TSV you must balance giving students the space to try things, such as doing research or writing policy, with providing the support and training needed to be successful. Yes, we want TSV to be student-led, but this does not mean being completely hands-off. We have seen examples where student-led teams ran into trouble with research question development because they skipped over root cause analysis, or they got into trouble with district leaders for not following internally defined protocols for communication. In both of these cases a more supportive adult mentor might have helped the youth avoid these problems. Note, this is not permission to take over a voice project—as we noted above, that would limit student engagement. Rather, work to be more of a partner with youth. The analogy of being a project manager can also be helpful in identifying some of the scaffolds you would offer as an adult leader of TSV.

Support Systems

Leading a student voice team can be difficult and emotionally draining. We have heard from multiple educators that having a system of emotional and practical support is helpful. It is more typical for student voice to exist in isolated classrooms; in contrast, a district office can bring together teachers to share best practices and to generally support each other through the ups and downs. In chapter 4, we mentioned that YL used a teacher training program. Though the goal of this program was curriculum development and teaching practice, many educators spoke about how the camaraderie and collaborative space helped to reenergize them.

Also in chapter 4, we discussed the role of relationships in scaling; the YL director having relationships with principals made it easier for her to leverage those relationships to assure support for both students and teachers. A supportive school leader can make the student voice process go more smoothly. In the vignette above, we saw that a school leader can be an impediment to student voice. However, we have also seen examples where a principal will meet monthly with their student voice team to hear the concerns of the team and provide resources to support their progress. Having such supports for teachers and TSV teams can help facilitate student voice in your school or district.

Youth-Adult Partnerships

Regardless of setting, the partnership between youth and adults is crucial to the success of TSV. In chapter 5, we described how TSV teachers saw their students as partners. We also shared the advice of being vulnerable with your students, sharing yourself in authentic ways, and incorporating community-building rituals. Not all adults will be interested in this type of relationship with youth, in which case you as a leader might have to screen out those educators who do not support student voice, as we described the YL director doing in chapter 4. Especially in short-term contacts, an adult who is condescending or unsupportive can do more damage than good.

A key aspect of youth-adult partnership is power sharing. In chapter 3, we described leadership roles for students in school and district improvement plans. In chapter 5, we highlighted various ways to develop leadership roles for youth in classrooms. For TSV to reach its fullest potential, power sharing is essential so that students have a stake in shaping the direction of their program and the ability to shape policy and practice.

Community Partnerships

You should resist the temptation of feeling like you have to go it alone in implementing your TSV program. Throughout the book we have addressed how partnerships can aid the development and growth of TSV. In chapters 4 and 6, we addressed the role of research-practice partnerships (RPP) between school districts and universities. In chapter 4, an RPP was instrumental in grant writing and program assessment that aided a school district in expanding the TSV program and documenting its impact. In chapter 6, we further discussed the potential of RPPs in TSV work. Although it is typical for university researchers to initiate RPPs, you as a district or school leader can also reach out to neighboring universities for researchers with matching interests or skills. Just remember: RPPs should be grounded in the practice needs and questions of your program and draw on the expertise of university partners, teachers, and students to address those needs.

In chapter 7, we looked at how school and community partnerships could elevate youth voice within a district. Here the promise comes from community organizations having recognized and respected standing with families. Findings produced in collaboration between a respected community organization and a school might be given more credibility in the community and with families. Community organizations might also have more experience with YPAR, providing school staff with helpful insights on how to create stronger student voice programming.

DOCUMENTING IMPACT AUTHENTICALLY

Students who experience TSV programs grow in a range of ways: they deepen their understanding of their own identities, develop new insight about social systems and institutions, develop critical consciousness, and build a host of skills for public leadership and social change, ranging from public speaking to peer organizing. These outcomes have been demonstrated in our prior work as well as in studies of similar kinds of transformative voice initiatives.[3] What's interesting about these student voice outcomes is that they are more *developmental* than *academic*. That is, they are part of a broader set of developmental tasks that are crucial to healthy adolescent development. What is unfortunately true is that these important skills do not always align with academic indicators, standardized test scores, or high school graduation requirements. This leaves the question of how to document the impact of TSV.

Now you might be inclined to say, why should we bother to document the outcomes of TSV type programs when we *know* that students exit these programs more empowered and better prepared to be civic actors in their community? In fact, at a recent student voice meeting, we engaged in just such a debate with teachers and students. One student in particular feared that assessing student voice would lead to more standardization—killing the spirit of student activism in the name of proving academic outcomes. While we get this point, we also understand the old adage that in schools, what gets assessed gets prioritized. Though we can argue whether pragmatism is sufficient reason to measure the impact in student voice work in schools, there is some truth to the fact that in schools or community organizations, if you cannot document the impact of a program, the program is at risk of being cut.

Though there may be no perfect way to navigate this tension between avoiding standardization and demonstrating outcomes, we think that *authentic assessment* offers the best path forward.[4] Authentic assessment can be a tool to document student learning and identify areas of relative weakness and strength in student voice programming. In the paragraphs that follow we briefly discuss the need for authentic assessment and provide an example of how to use authentic assessment to document program outcomes.

Most schools will rely on standardized assessment to measure student outcomes. A standardized assessment might be efficacious in measuring knowledge in mathematics or history—where there is a predetermined knowledge base that students are expected to attain. When youth engage in TSV, they partake in a form of open-ended inquiry. Yes, there might be some shared experiences like developing teamwork skills, learning to lead a group of peers, engaging in root cause analysis, selecting appropriate research methodologies, or making a policy argument. However, because of the uniqueness of each student group's experience, they will select a unique issue, research methodology, and approach to policymaking. This makes it particularly challenging to develop a standardized assessment that will work across contexts.

Instead, we argue for the use of authentic assessment with TSV. Authentic assessments are meant to mirror real-world skills; they assess the degree to which students master and execute skills necessary in life, such as persuasive argumentation or leadership skills. An example of an authentic assessment that we use in TSV is the Measure of Youth Policy Arguments (MYPA).[5] MYPA was designed to assess the efficacy of students in delivering convincing policy arguments. The beauty of MYPA is that it does not rely on the memorization of facts, instead it examines how well students can give a persuasive policy argument, including developing a compelling introduction, using evidence to support one's argument, and presenting a call to action from your audience—all of which are skills which students can use into adult life.

In recent years, our partners from YL (whom we introduced you to in chapter 4) have given increasing thought as to how to authentically assess student outcomes. In the past they have relied on survey results that documented improvement in student outcomes such as civic self-efficacy, critical thinking, and perceived relevance of school. While these findings were positive in demonstrating student growth related to academic and social-emotional behaviors, the results did not directly align with their district's defined student competencies. As such, YL staff are rethinking how to measure student outcomes. They are driven by a desire to demonstrate how students are attaining desired competencies and also to provide YL teachers with a way to grade and give feedback to students. To this end, we are supporting YL in the process of designing a formative classroom assessment and a programwide, more summative assessment. Though the process of developing an authentic assessment can be rather arduous, below are some basic considerations.

Developing a Scoring Rubric for Authentic Assessments

- Identify the key outcomes you wish your students to demonstrate. For these, you might look at your mission or vision statement. We have worked with programs that were interested in assessing their students' critical analytical skills, ability to conduct research, and ability to deliver persuasive policy arguments. Consider engaging with key stakeholders such as teachers, students, and community members.
- Consider how a young person would demonstrate that they possess each of the key outcomes. What are the substeps that go into reaching the big outcome? It is possible that you might have to have multiple items to assess a given outcome. For example, with the research outcome, you might want separate items that look at whether students know how to develop research questions, know of different methodologies, know how to conduct data analysis, and know how to derive findings.
- Continue to develop individual items that get at each of the remaining key outcomes.
- It is key to differentiate a high level of mastery from lower levels. Back to the example of research skills, what would it look like for a student to show a high level of ability in deriving research findings? Maybe it is something like: *uses outcomes from research to make conclusions.* Sometimes it can be helpful to have a counterexample (to show what the baseline level of understanding is). In this case a counterexample might be: *derives a conclusion that does not consider research findings.*
- Once you have a draft, try out your assessment. Does it give you the results you anticipated? Are the results helpful, and do they align with how you would have rated a student without the assessment? If not, go back and tweak the assessment. Also consider if your assessment is easy to use. Ideally, you could hand it off to a colleague, and they would be able to use it with minimal training.

Aside from authentic assessments, there are other ways to demonstrate the impact of your TSV program. Consider school-level data like attendance, disciplinary infractions, and graduation rates. Track this data for your TSV participants. This is not a perfect measure of program success, obviously, because any number of things can impact attendance and grade point average. But if your students are showing better graduation rates, or over time your students have better attendance, then you can make the argument that your TSV program is having an impact. Something we have seen anecdotally in our own work is that youth who participate in TSV grow in their level of engagement in school. They are generally more confident in their academic ability and are better able to advocate for their needs.

Finally, consider collecting testimonials from your participants. In schools there is definitely a bias toward quantitative data. However, the words of young people can be a powerful tool in telling the story of TSV, particularly when sharing how the experience has impacted them. See the following example from Alegria, a former student, describing what she learned through her participation in a TSV program.

Alegria's Testimonial

I've learned a lot. I think the biggest thing—okay, not the biggest thing, but one of the first things I learned is to not be shy in any space ... you're obviously there for a reason. You're there to contribute something that others can't contribute or speak on ... So just know that you're there for a reason, and don't be afraid to speak out and reach out to others. Because at first I was really—I'm a reserved person, but talk to everyone else. Talk to the other student leaders because combining powers is just the best thing you can do. It's honest fun, you know? It gives you energy.

While student testimonials might not be considered hard evidence of a program's success, they can be helpful in demonstrating the richness of student outcomes.

PARTING THOUGHTS

There is an infectious energy when young people claim their voice and use it to impact their schools and community. As an adult, even when you are only an ally or accomplice to this work, you can't help but share in this high. Maybe you have picked up on the glimmer of this feeling as you have read through this book. We know that retelling these stories has boosted both our spirits and our resolve to spread this work to more schools.

Though there are elements of this work that at times seem magical or hard to visualize in the practice, the basics of TSV are simple. They are grounded in humanism, a belief in the ability of youth, a desire to treat education's major stakeholders as respected contributors, and a realization that exercising one's voice can be both empowering and healing. We are also grounded in the belief that when youth contribute their voice to schools, they positively impact educators and school systems themselves. To this end there is an easy starting point, one that we have heard in student interviews through our many years of research; it is voiced here by Camelia. We specifically asked Camelia at her end-of-year interview what advice she would give to adults who wanted to support student voice. She said:

Camelia's Testimonial

The only thing I would say is to support us. At the end of the day, regardless if we're a child, a kid, we're going to make it happen and we just want to be supported by people who think it can happen too. Because there some people who don't believe in the same things we do, which is fine, but at the end of the day, support goes a long way.

Evidence of Student Voice Impacts

IN THIS APPENDIX, we highlight research evidence, focused on studies in the United States, on the impact of student voice for student learning and motivation and school change. This may be helpful to you as you build your plan and develop support from board members or others who want to see the evidence that student voice works.

> *Student voice: when young people experience opportunities to influence decisions about policies and practices in their classrooms and schools.*

Student Voice Is Supported by Research on Adolescent Learning and Development

- Student voice enables young people to exercise agency and self-determination, which are central to intrinsic motivation and academic engagement.[1]

- Student voice enables experiences of open-ended decision-making, judgment, and planning, all essential for the development of the teen brain.[2]
- Student voice encourages student-teacher relationships, which are central to motivation, engagement, and belonging.[3]

Research on Student Voice Shows Positive Outcomes for Student Learning, Student Engagement, and School Reform

- Students have better grades and attendance and reduced rates of absenteeism in schools that are responsive to student voice and critiques.[4]
- Students in a program that combined student voice, ethnic studies, and participatory action research were more likely to pass standardized tests and graduate from high school.[5]
- Collegial interaction with adults helps participants to develop new forms of social and cultural capital.[6]
- Experiences of voice and agency for minoritized students are associated with stronger ethnic identity and an increased perception that school is relevant.[7]
- Opportunities to engage in critical social analysis of the world are associated with academic engagement for minoritized students.[8]
- By giving input into their curriculum, students experience authentic learning about issues relevant to their lives and aspirations.[9]
- Experiences of voice, feedback, and choice in the classroom contribute to academic engagement, competence, and belonging in the classroom.[10]
- Schools that create space for all students to provide their perspectives, share in decision-making, and lead and initiate action promote social and emotional learning.[11]
- Students who experience structured student voice opportunities experience growth in critical reflection abilities,

political efficacy, engagement in sociopolitical action, and leadership skills.[12]

- Formal roles for students to work with adults on school decision-making and improvement lead to better school reform outcomes that are more likely to be sustained.[13]
- Student-led action research enabled students to influence curricular and climate-related policies and practices at school.[14]

If you are interested in doing your own research on outcomes tied to student voice programming, check out a new set of student voice survey resources hosted by the Search Institute.[15]

Building Your Team

IN THIS APPENDIX, we provide a set of vignettes that you might use in interviews as you create your team or select adults to engage in student voice work with students—these can also be good conversations for you to have within your teams as you solidify your communication plan.

INTERVIEW QUESTIONS

When interviewing members of your student voice team, you are trying to understand how they think about the role of adults and students, about respect, and about the purpose of school. Consider sharing the following scenarios and quotes with your potential team members, and conduct your interview as a discussion of the scenario or quote.

- We are going to be starting a student voice team, where students will work with adults to identify problems, research those issues, and propose solutions. What is your reaction to that idea? How would you define student voice?

[For the adults:] Tell me about a time when a student gave you feedback. How did you respond?

■ Richard Shaull, in his foreword to Paulo Freire's *Pedagogy of the Oppressed*, said:

> Education either functions as an instrument that is used to facilitate the integration of the younger generation into the logic of the present system and bring about conformity to it, or it becomes 'the practice of freedom,' the means by which men and women deal critically and creatively with reality and discover how to participate in the transformation of their world.[1]

What is your reaction to that quote? What is the purpose of education from *your* perspective? What do you do in your classroom, or work, that shows that purpose?

■ Deborah Roseman (@roseperson) reposted this statement on X (August 27, 2019):

> Sometimes people use "respect" to mean "treating someone like a person" and sometimes they use "respect" to mean "treating someone like an authority" and sometimes people who are used to being treated like an authority say "if you won't respect me I won't respect you" and they mean "if you won't treat me like an authority I won't treat you like a person" and they think they're being fair but they aren't and it's not okay.

What is your reaction to that statement? How do you define *respect*?[2]

■ This quote is from a classroom management consultant:

> The number one rule in my classroom is to "Be Respectful; Obey the First Time Without Arguing or Talking Back." All of my students are familiar with my rules and they know that I will not tolerate back talk. So, when I respond, it is to either tell the student not to talk back

(give a warning) or to send the student to the hallway, immediately, because s/he crossed the line into belligerence and/or a temper tantrum. I am not perfect, I make mistakes, and I teach my students that if they don't agree with me they can talk to me after class. This behavior, "talking back," is the student's attempt to manipulate the teacher in order to get out of trouble and/or to get his/her way. It is not respectful to argue with the teacher or pitch fits. Period.[3]

What is your reaction to this rule? What would you say to a colleague if you heard them say this? What if a student told you a teacher said this to them? How would you advise them?

- Two of the biggest challenges in student voice work are the fear of critique and the fear of failure. Often educators worry that they will experience retaliation, or poor evaluations, or angry parents, or maybe make the cafeteria staff angry. Or they worry that the young people will come up with great ideas, do good work, propose good solutions, and not get what they ask for—that their work might be dismissed or ignored. Tell me about your fears related to student voice work, and especially about these ideas of critique and failure.

Notes

Chapter 1

1. Robert V. Bullough, "Refocusing the Agenda of Public Education: District Mission Statements and the Manners of Democracy as a Way of Life," *Democracy and Education* 30, no. 2, article 3 (October 2022), https://democracyeducationjournal.org/home/vol30/iss2/3/.
2. Kai A. Schafft and Catharine Biddle, "Place and Purpose in Public Education: School District Mission Statements and Educational (Dis) Embeddedness," *American Journal of Education* 120, no. 1 (November 2013): 55–76, https://doi.org/10.1086/673173.
3. Steven E. Stemler, Damian Bebell, and Lauren Ann Sonnabend, "Using School Mission Statements for Reflection and Research," *Educational Administration Quarterly* 47, no. 2 (April 2011): 383–420, https://doi.org/10.1177/0013161X10387590.
4. Schafft and Biddle, "Place and Purpose."
5. Shelley Zion and Sheryl Petty, "Student Voices in Urban School and District Improvement: Creating Youth-Adult Partnerships for Student Success and Social Justice," in *Ability, Equity, and Culture: Sustaining Inclusive Urban Education Reform*, ed. Elizabeth B. Kozleski and Kathleen King Thorius (New York: Teachers College Press, 2013), 35–62; Dana Mitra, Stephanie Serriere, and Ben Kirshner, "Youth Participation in U.S. Contexts: Student Voice Without a National Mandate," *Children and Society* 28, no. 4 (July 2014): 292–304, https://doi.org/10.1111/chso.12005; Alison Cook-Sather, "Authorizing Students' Perspectives: Toward Trust, Dialogue, and Change in Education," *Educational Researcher* 31, no. 4 (May 2002): 3–14, https://www.jstor.org/stable/3594363; Dave Bechtel and Cynthia Reed, "Students as Documenters: Benefits, Reflections, and Suggestions," *NASSP* 82, no. 594 (January 1998): 89–95, https://doi.org/10.1177/019263659808259413; Frederick Erickson and Jeffrey

Shultz, "Students' Experience of the Curriculum," in *Handbook of Research on Curriculum: A Project of the American Educational Research Association*, ed. Philip W. Jackson (New York: MacMillan Publishing Company, 1992), 465–87.

6. Jeff Walls and Samantha E. Holquist, "Through Their Eyes, in Their Words: Using Photo-Elicitation to Amplify Student Voice in Policy and School Improvement Research," in *Research Methods for Social Justice and Equity in Education*, ed. Kamden K. Strunk and Leslie Ann Locke (Gewerbestrasse, Switzerland: Palgrave Macmillan, 2019), 151–161.

7. Shelley Zion, "Transformative Student Voice: Extending the Role of Youth in Addressing Systemic Marginalization in U.S. Schools," *Multiple Voices: Disability, Race, and Language Intersections in Special Education* 20, no. 1 (Spring 2020): 32–43, https://doi.org/10.56829/2158-396X-20.1.32; Carol Robinson and Carol Taylor, "Theorizing Student Voice: Values and Perspectives," *Improving Schools* 10, no. 1 (March 2007): 5–17, https://doi.org/10.1177/1365480207073702.

8. Charles M. Reigeluth, "The Imperative for Systemic Change," in *Systemic Change in Education*, ed. Charles M. Reigeluth and Robert J. Garfinkle (Englewood Cliffs, NJ: Educational Technology Publications, 1994), 172.

9. Patricia Hill Collins, *Black Feminist Thought: Knowledge, Consciousness, and the Politics of Empowerment* (New York: Routledge, 1991).

10. Paulo Freire, *Pedagogy of the Oppressed* (New York: Continuum, 1970), 34.

11. Béla H. Bánáthy, *Designing Social Systems in a Changing World* (New York: Plenum Press, 1996), vii.

12. Carlos P. Hipolito-Delgado et al., "Transformative Student Voice for Sociopolitical Development: Developing Youth of Color as Political Actors," *Research on Adolescence* 32, no. 3 (September 2022): 1098–1108, https://doi.org/10.1111/jora.12753; Ben Kirshner et al., "A Theory of Change for Scaling Critical Civic Inquiry," *Peabody Journal of Education* 96, no. 3 (2021): 294–306, https://doi.org/10.1080/0161956X.2021.1942708; Shepherd Zeldin, Linda Camino, and Carrie Mook, "The Adoption of Innovation in Youth Organizations: Creating the Conditions for Youth–Adult Partnerships," *Journal of Community Psychology* 33, no. 1 (January 2005): 121–35, https://doi.org/10.1002/jcop.20044.

13. Carlos P. Hipolito-Delgado and Shelley Zion, "Igniting the Fire Within Marginalized Youth: The Role of Critical Civic Inquiry in Fostering Ethnic Identity and Civic Self-Efficacy," *Urban Education* 52, no. 6 (July 2017): 699–717, https://doi.org/10.1177/0042085915574524;

Ben Kirshner, *Youth Activism in an Era of Education Inequality* (New York: New York University Press, 2015); Zion, "Transformative Student Voice."

14. Roderick J. Watts and Constance Flanagan, "Pushing the Envelope on Youth Civic Engagement: A Developmental and Liberation Psychology Perspective," *Journal of Community Psychology* 35, no. 6 (August 2007): 779–92, https://doi.org/10.1002/jcop.20178.

15. Freire, *Pedagogy of the Oppressed*.

16. Orlando Fals-Borda, "The Application of Participatory Action-Research in Latin America," *International Sociology* 2, no. 4 (December 1987): 329–47, https://doi.org/10.1177/026858098700200401; Freire, *Pedagogy of the Oppressed*; Julio Cammarota and Michelle Fine, *Revolutionizing Education: Youth Participatory Action Research in Motion* (New York: Routledge, 2008); Jason Irizarry, "Buscando la Libertad: Latino Youths in Search of Freedom in School," *Democracy and Education* 19, no. 1, article 4 (2011), https://democracyeducationjournal.org/home/vol19/iss1/4.

17. Ben Kirshner, Carlos P. Hipolito-Delgado, and Shelley Zion, "Sociopolitical Development in Educational Systems: From Margins to Center,"*Urban Review* 47, no. 5 (December 2015): 803–808, http://doi.org/10.1007/s11256-015-0335-8.

18. Shelley Zion et al., "Urban Schooling and the Transformative Possibilities of Participatory Action Research: The Role of Youth in Struggles for Urban Education Justice," in *Handbook of Urban Education*, 2nd ed., ed. H. Richard Milner IV and Kofi Lomotey (New York: Routledge, 2021), 507–22; Angela Booker, "Contingent Authority and Youth Influence: When Youth Councils Can Wield Influence in Public Institutions," *Revista de Investigación Educativa* 35, no. 2 (June 2017): 537–62, https://doi.org/10.6018/rie.35.2.274841; Irizarry, "Buscando la Libertad."

19. Julio Cammarota, "A Social Justice Approach to Achievement: Guiding Latina/o Students Toward Educational Attainment with a Challenging, Socially Relevant Curriculum," *Equity and Excellence in Education* 40, no. 1 (February 2007): 87–96, https://doi.org/10.1080/10665680601015153; Mariah Kornbluh et al., "Youth Participatory Action Research as an Approach to Sociopolitical Development and the New Academic Standards: Considerations for Educators," *Urban Review* 47, no. 5 (December 2015): 868–92, https://doi.org/10.1007/s11256-015-0337-6.

20. Nolan L. Cabrera et al., "Missing the (Student Achievement) Forest for All the (Political) Trees: Empiricism and the Mexican American

Studies Controversy in Tucson," *American Educational Research Journal* 51, no. 6 (December 2014): 1084–1118, https://doi.org/10.3102/0002831214553705; Scott Seider and Daren Graves, *Schooling for Critical Consciousness: Engaging Black and Latinx Youth in Analyzing, Navigating, and Challenging Racial Injustice* (Cambridge, MA: Harvard Education Press, 2020); Aaliyah El-Amin et al., "Critical Consciousness: A Key to Student Achievement," *Phi Delta Kappan* 98, no. 5 (February 2017): 18–23, https://doi.org/10.1177/0031721717690360.

21. Hipolito-Delgado et al., "Transformative Student Voice for Sociopolitical Development"; Parissa J. Ballard, Alison K. Cohen, and Joshua Littenberg-Tobias, "Action Civics for Promoting Civic Development: Main Effects of Program Participation and Differences by Project Characteristics," *American Journal of Community Psychology* 58, nos. 3–4 (December 2016): 377–90, https://doi.org/10.1002/ajcp.12103; Cabrera et al., "Missing the (Student Achievement) Forest"; Cammarota, "A Social Justice Approach"; Rosario Ceballo, Marisela Huerta, and Quyen Epstein-Ngo, "Parental and School Influences Promoting Academic Success Among Latino Students," in *Handbook of Research on Schools, Schooling, and Human Development*, ed. Judith L. Meece and Jacquelynne S. Eccles (New York: Routledge, 2010), 293–307; Dana L. Mitra, "The Significance of Students: Can Increasing 'Student Voice' in Schools Lead to Gains in Youth Development?" *Teachers College Record* 106, no. 4 (April 2004): 651–88, https://doi.org/10.1111/j.1467-9620.2004.00354.x; Irizarry, "Buscando la Libertad."

22. Kirshner et al., "A Theory of Change"; Zion, "Transformative Student Voice."

23. Hipolito-Delgado and Zion, "Igniting the Fire"; Kirshner, *Youth Activism*.

24. Kirshner, *Youth Activism*.

25. Zion and Petty, "Student Voices."

26. Shelley Zion, Carrie D. Allen, and Christina Jean, "Enacting a Critical Pedagogy, Influencing Teachers' Sociopolitical Development," *Urban Review* 47, no. 5 (December 2015): 914–933, https://doi.org/10.1007/s11256-015-0340-y.

27. Shelley Zion, Adam York, and Dane Stickney, "Bound Together: White Teachers/Latinx Students Revising Resistance," in *The Power of Resistance: Culture, Ideology and Social Reproduction in Global Contexts*, ed. Rowhea M. Elmesky, Carol Camp Yeakey, and Olivia Marcucci (Bingley, UK: Emerald Publishing, 2017), 429–58; Kirshner, Hipolito-Delgado, and Zion, "Sociopolitical Dimensions."

28. Barbara Rogoff, *The Cultural Nature of Human Development* (New York: Oxford University Press, 2003).

29. Daniela K. DiGiacomo, "Relational Equity by Design: Insights from the Kentucky Student Voice Team and Their Adult Research Ally" (under review).

30. Shepherd Zeldin, Brian D. Christens, and Jane L. Powers, "The Psychology and Practice of Youth-Adult Partnership: Bridging Generations for Youth Development and Community Change," *American Journal of Community Psychology* 51, nos. 3–4 (June 2013): 385–97, https://doi.org/10.1007/s10464-012-9558-y.

31. Zeldin, Christens, and Powers, "Psychology and Practice."

32. Zion and Petty, "Student Voices."

33. Zion and Petty, "Student Voices."

34. Roderick J. Watts, Derek M. Griffith, and Jaleel Abdul-Adil, "Sociopolitical Development as an Antidote for Oppression—Theory and Action," *American Journal of Community Psychology* 27, no. 2 (April 1999): 255–71, https://doi.org/10.1023/A:1022839818873; Roderick J. Watts, Nat Chioke Williams, and Robert J. Jagers, "Sociopolitical Development," *American Journal of Community Psychology* 31, nos. 1–2 (March 2003): 185–94, https://doi.org/10.1023/A:1023091024140.

35. Zion, Allen, and Jean, "Enacting a Critical Pedagogy."

36. Bánáthy, *Designing Social Systems*.

37. Zion et al., "Urban Schooling"; Michelle Renée, Kevin Welner, and Jeannie Oakes, "Social Movement Organizing and Equity-Focused Educational Change: Shifting the Zone of Mediation," in *Second International Handbook of Educational Change*, ed. Andy Hargreaves et al. (New York: Springer, 2010), 153–68.

38. Reigeluth, "The Imperative for Systemic Change" Amelia Peterson et al., "Making Human-Centered Systems Design Work in Education," *Education Week* (blog), February 3, 2016, https://www.edweek.org/leadership/opinion-making-human-centered-systems-design-work-in-education/2016/02; Charles M. Reigeluth, "Teacher Empowerment, Student Choice, and Equity in School Districts: A Non-Bureaucratic Alternative for School Organization and Accountability," preprint, ResearchGate, August 2018, https://www.researchgate.net/publication/330761366.

39. Zion, "Transformative Student Voice."

40. Hipolito-Delgado et al., "Transformative Student Voice for Sociopolitical Development"; Carlos P. Hipolito-Delgado et al., "Fostering Youth Sociopolitical Action: The Roles of Critical Reflection,

Sociopolitical Efficacy, and Transformative Student Voice," *Urban Education* 59, no. 4 (April 2024, published online December 2021): 1132–58, https://doi.org/10.1177/00420859211068468.

41. Hipolito-Delgado and Zion, "Igniting the Fire."
42. Hipolito-Delgado and Zion, "Igniting the Fire"; Kirshner, *Youth Activism*.
43. Zion, York, and Stickney, "Bound Together"; Zion, Allen, and Jean, "Enacting a Critical Pedagogy."
44. Zion and Petty, "Student Voices"; Zion, "Transformative Student Voice."
45. Kirshner et al., "A Theory of Change."
46. Kirshner, *Youth Activism*; Zion, York, and Stickney, "Bound Together."
47. Dane Stickney et al., *Transformative Student Voice: A Guide to Classroom Action* (Cambridge, MA: Harvard Education Press, forthcoming 2025).
48. Cook-Sather, "Authorizing Students' Perspectives," x.

Chapter 2

1. "Consensus Decision Making: A Short Guide," Seeds for Change, https://www.seedsforchange.org.uk/shortconsensus.
2. "Setting Group Agreements with Youth," Heart-Mind Online, https://heartmindonline.org/resources/setting-group-agreements-with-youth.
3. Michelle Molitor and Nicole Young, "Why Start with Agreements?," *The Equity Lab* (blog), https://www.theequitylab.org/blog/why-start-with-agreements.
4. Other major districts have made similar commitments: Chicago Public Schools has a Department of Student Voice and Engagement. The Minneapolis Public School District's Department of Research, Evaluation and Assessment operates a Youth Participatory Evaluation program, in which students "gather information from others in the school, figure out what's working and what's not working, and make recommendations about what needs to change."
5. John Bell, *Understanding Adultism: A Major Obstacle to Developing Positive Youth-Adult Relationships* (Somerville, MA: YouthBuild USA, March 1995), https://actioncivics.scoe.net/pdf/Understanding_Adultism.pdf.

Chapter 3

1. Other scholars of student voice have proposed similar frameworks, including the language of a pyramid or levels, to distinguish different types of student voice. The pyramid we propose here is based on

Shelley's analysis of data from research carried out in the Rural Schools Project. For similar frameworks, see Dana Mitra, "Increasing Student Voice and Moving Toward Youth Leadership," *Prevention Researcher* 13, no. 1 (January 2005): 7–10; Dane Stickney and Julissa Ventura, "Possibilities of Student Voice," *Phi Delta Kappan* 105, no. 8 (May 1, 2024): 14–19, https://doi.org/10.1177/00317217241251876; Ginnie Logan, "Student Voice—Transformative or Symbolic?" Students at the Center Hub, September 30, 2019, https://studentsatthe-centerhub.org/resource/student-voice-transformative-symbolic/; Eric Toshalis and Michael J. Nakkula, Motivation, Engagement, and Student Voice, Students at the Center Series (Boston: Jobs for the Future, April 2012), https://www.howyouthlearn.org/pdf/Motivation%20 Engagement%20Student%20Voice_0.pdf.

Chapter 4

1. Mariah Kornbluh et al., "Youth Participatory Action Research as an Approach to Sociopolitical Development and the New Academic Standards: Considerations for Educators," *Urban Review* 47, no. 5 (December 2015): 868–92, https://doi.org/10.1007/s11256-015-0337 -6; Peter Levine and Kei Kawashima-Ginsberg, "Preparing for Civic Life," in *Rethinking Readiness: Deeper Learning for College, Work, and Life*, ed. Rafael Heller, Rebecca C. Wolfe, and Adria Steinberg (Cambridge, MA: Harvard Education Press, 2017).

2. Van T. Lac and Katherine Cumings Mansfield, "What Do Students Have to Do with Educational Leadership? Making a Case for Centering Student Voice," *Journal of Research on Leadership Education* 13, no. 1 (March 2018): 38–58, https://doi.org/10.1177/1942775117743748; Jason D. Salisbury, Manali J. Sheth, and Alexia Angton, "'They Didn't Even Talk About Oppression': School Leadership Protecting the Whiteness of Leadership Through Resistance Practices to a Youth Voice Initiative," *Journal of Education Human Resources* 38, no. 1 (Winter 2020): 57–81, https://doi.org/10.3138/jehr.2019-0010.

3. Melanie Bertrand, Maneka Deanna Brooks, and Ashley D. Domínguez, "Challenging Adultism: Centering Youth as Educational Decision Makers," *Urban Education* 58, no. 10 (December 2023): 2570–97, https://doi.org/10.1177/0042085920959135.

4. Ben Kirshner, *Youth Activism in an Era of Education Inequality* (New York: New York University Press, 2015).

5. Gerry Czerniawski, "Repositioning Trust: A Challenge to Inauthentic Neoliberal Uses of Pupil Voice," *Management in Education* 26, no. 3 (July 2012): 130–39, https://doi.org/10.1177/0892020612445685.

6. Jerusha O. Conner, "Pawns or Power Players: The Grounds on Which Adults Dismiss or Defend Youth Organizers in the USA," *Journal of Youth Studies* 19, no. 3 (2016): 403–20, https://doi.org/10.1080/13676261.2015.1083958.

7. Lac and Mansfield, "What Do Students Have to Do?"

8. Bertrand, Brooks, and Domínguez, "Challenging Adultism"; Conner, "Pawns or Power Players."

9. Jerusha O. Conner, C. Nathan Ober, and Amanda S. Brown, "The Politics of Paternalism: Adult and Youth Perspectives on Youth Voice in Public Policy," *Teachers College Record* 118, no. 8 (August 2016): 1–48, https://doi.org/10.1177/016146811611800805; Ginnie Logan, "Student Voice—Transformative or Symbolic?" Students at the Center Hub, September 30, 2019, https://studentsatthecenterhub.org/resource/student-voice-transformative-symbolic.

10. Conner, "Pawns or Power Players"; Czerniawski, "Repositioning Trust."

11. Kirshner, *Youth Activism*.

12. Christopher J. Buttimer, "The Challenges and Possibilities of Youth Participatory Action Research for Teachers and Students in Public School Classrooms," *Berkeley Review of Education* 8, no. 1 (Fall/Winter 2018): 39–81, https://doi.org/10.5070/B88133830.

13. Dane Stickney et al., *Transformative Student Voice for Teachers: A Guide to Classroom Action* (Cambridge, MA: Harvard Education Press, forthcoming 2025).

14. Carlos P. Hipolito-Delgado and Shelley Zion, "Igniting the Fire Within Marginalized Youth: The Role of Critical Civic Inquiry in Fostering Ethnic Identity and Civic Self-Efficacy," *Urban Education* 52, no. 6 (July 2017): 699–717, https://doi.org/10.1177/0042085915574524.

15. Carlos P. Hipolito-Delgado et al., "Transformative Student Voice for Sociopolitical Development: Developing Youth of Color as Political Actors," *Research on Adolescence* 32, no. 3 (September 2022): 1098–1108, https://doi.org/10.1111/jora.12753.

16. Dane Stickney, Elizabeth Milligan Cordova, and Carlos P. Hipolito-Delgado, "Get Out of Your Own Way: Sharing Power to Engage Students of Color in Authentic Conversations of Social Inequity," in *Making Classroom Discussions Work: Methods for Quality Dialogue in the Social Studies*, ed. Jane C. Lo (New York: Teachers College Press, 2022), 176–91.

Chapter 5

1. Carlos P. Hipolito-Delgado and Shelley Zion, "Igniting the Fire Within Marginalized Youth: The Role of Critical Civic Inquiry in Fostering

Ethnic Identity and Civic Self-Efficacy," *Urban Education* 52, no. 6 (July 2017): 699–717, https://doi.org/10.1177/0042085915574524; Ben Kirshner, *Youth Activism in an Era of Education Inequality* (New York: New York University Press, 2015).

2. Nicole Mirra, Antero Garcia, and Ernest Morrell, *Doing Youth Participatory Action Research: Transforming Inquiry with Researchers, Educators, and Students* (New York: Routledge, 2016); Limarys Caraballo et al., "YPAR and Critical Epistemologies: Rethinking Education Research," *Review of Research in Education* 41, no. 1 (March 2017): 311–36, https://doi.org/10.3102/0091732X16686948; Daniel Morales-Doyle and Alejandra Frausto, "Youth Participatory Science: A Grassroots Science Curriculum Framework," *Educational Action Research* 29, no. 1 (2021): 60–78, https://doi.org/10.1080/09650792.2019.1706598.

3. Dane Stickney, "Awareness, Knowledge, Action: One Middle-School Classroom's Journey to Empowerment," Students at the Center Hub, September 6, 2019, https://studentsatthecenterhub.org/resource/middle-school-classrooms-journey-empowerment.

4. Lyn Mikel Brown, Catharine Biddle, and Mark Tappan, *Trauma-Responsive Schooling: Centering Student Voice and Healing* (Cambridge, MA: Harvard Education Press, 2022); Joseph A. Durlak et al., "The Impact of Enhancing Students' Social and Emotional Learning: A Meta-Analysis of School-Based Universal Interventions," *Child Development* 82, no. 1 (January–February 2011): 405–32, https://doi.org/10.1111/j.1467-8624.2010.01564.x; Jacquelynne S. Eccles and Robert W. Roeser, "School and Community Influences on Human Development," in *Developmental Science: An Advanced Textbook*, 6th ed., ed. Marc H. Bornstein and Michael E. Lamb (New York: Psychology Press, 2011), 571–644; Carol D. Lee, Andrew N. Meltzoff, and Patricia K. Kuhl, "The Braid of Human Learning and Development," in *Handbook of the Cultural Foundations of Learning*, ed. Na'ilah Suad Nasir et al. (New York: Routledge, 2020).

5. Shepherd Zeldin, Brian D. Christens, and Jane L. Powers, "The Psychology and Practice of Youth-Adult Partnership: Bridging Generations for Youth Development and Community Change," *American Journal of Community Psychology* 51, nos. 3–4 (June 2013): 385–97, https://doi.org/10.1007/s10464-012-9558-y.

6. Carlos P. Hipolito-Delgado et al., "Fostering Youth Sociopolitical Action: The Roles of Critical Reflection, Sociopolitical Efficacy, and Transformative Student Voice," *Urban Education* 59, no. 4 (April 2024, published online December 2021): 1132–58, https://doi.org/10.1177/00420859211068468.

7. Angela Valenzuela, *Subtractive Schooling: U.S.-Mexican Youth and the Politics of Caring* (New York: State University of New York Press, 1999).

8. Priya Parmar and Shirley Steinberg, "Locating Yourself for Your Students," in *Everyday Antiracism: Getting Real About Race in School*, ed. Mica Pollock (New York: The New Press, 2008), 287–90.

9. Eric DeMeulenaere, "Toward a Pedagogy of Trust," in *High-Expectation Curricula: Helping All Students Succeed with Powerful Learning*, ed. Curt Dudley-Marling and Sarah Michaels (New York: Teachers College Press, 2012): 28–41.

10. DeMeulenaere, "Toward a Pedagogy."

11. Victor Battistich, "School Contexts That Promote Students' Positive Development," in *Handbook of Research on Schools, Schooling, and Human Development*, ed. Judith L. Meece and Jacquelynne S. Eccles (New York: Routledge, 2010): 111–27.

12. Jean Piaget, *The Moral Judgment of the Child* (New York: Routledge, 1999).

13. Ben Kirshner, *Youth Activism in an Era of Education Inequality* (New York: New York University Press, 2015).

14. Shelley D. Zion, "Systems, Stakeholders, and Students: Including Students in School Reform," *Improving Schools* 12, no. 2 (July 2009): 131–43, https://doi.org/10.1177/1365480209105577; Dennis Thiessen and Alison Cook-Sather, eds., *International Handbook of Student Experience in Elementary and Secondary School* (Dordrecht, Netherlands: Springer, 2007).

15. Paulo Freire, *Pedagogy of the Oppressed* (New York: Continuum, 1970).

16. Nolan L. Cabrera et al., "Missing the (Student Achievement) Forest for All the (Political) Trees: Empiricism and the Mexican American Studies Controversy in Tucson," *American Educational Research Journal* 51, no. 6 (December 2014): 1084–1118, https://doi.org/10.3102/0002831214553705; Scott Seider and Daren Graves, *Schooling for Critical Consciousness: Engaging Black and Latinx Youth in Analyzing, Navigating, and Challenging Racial Injustice* (Cambridge, MA: Harvard Education Press, 2020); Aaliyah El-Amin et al., "Critical Consciousness: A Key to Student Achievement," *Phi Delta Kappan* 98, no. 5 (February 2017): 18–23, https://doi.org/10.1177/0031721717690360.

17. Facing History & Ourselves website, accessed July 7, 2024, https://www.facinghistory.org.

18. Julio Cammarota, "A Social Justice Approach to Achievement: Guiding Latina/o Students Toward Educational Attainment with a Challenging, Socially Relevant Curriculum," *Equity and Excellence in*

Education 40, no. 1 (February 2007): 87–96, https://doi.org/10.1080/10665680601015153.

19. Street Law website, accessed July 3, 2024, https://streetlaw.org.

20. Curriculum specialists and statistics professors from the Education Development Center developed two curriculum modules: "Investigating Income Inequality in the U.S." and "Investigating Immigration to the U.S.," each of which start with social justice topics, address standards-based content, and use sophisticated, publicly available digital tools to analyze large-scale data sets. Both can be found at "Investigating U.S. Society with Data (USS-DATA)," USS-DATA, https://sites.google.com/view/uss-data/home. The Coachella Valley [California] School District, known for its early adoption and development of rigorous ethnic studies curricula, has published twelfth-grade statistics units that engage students in quantitative reasoning to understand social issues. Other resources that we recommend build on the work of Rico Gutstein, who is a leading scholar of social justice approaches to math instruction: Josephine Louie et al., "Advancing Social Justice Learning Through Data Literacy," *ASCD* (blog), May 1, 2023, https://www.ascd.org/el/articles/advancing-social-justice-learning-through-data-literacy; and Eric (Rico) Gutstein and Bob Peterson, eds., *Rethinking Mathematics: Teaching Social Justice by the Numbers* (Milwaukee, WI: Rethinking Schools, 2006). The latter includes multiple case examples and curriculum examples relevant to a high school class. Although statistics instruction offers the most common example of using math to learn about social issues, we suggest that interested teachers and department heads explore related resources for algebra: (Robert P. Moses and Charles E. Cobb Jr., *Radical Equations: Civil Rights from Mississippi to the Algebra Project* (Boston: Beacon Press, 2001); and geometry: Jonathan Osler's RadicalMath website, https://www.radicalmath.org, has examples using geometry tools to map neighborhoods and proximity to toxins.

21. "inquiryHub: Research-Based Curricula Supporting Next Generation Science," University of Colorado Boulder, accessed July 2024, https://www.colorado.edu/program/inquiryhub/curricula.

22. Morales-Doyle and Frausto, "Youth Participatory Science."

23. Eve Tuck, "Suspending Damage: A Letter to Communities," *Harvard Educational Review* 79, no. 3 (September 2009): 409–28, https://doi.org/10.17763/haer.79.3.n0016675661t3n15; Morales-Doyle and Frausto, "Youth Participatory Science," 67.

24. National Research Council, *Engaging Schools: Fostering High School Students' Motivation to Learn* (Washington, DC: National Academies

Press, 2004), https://doi.org/10.17226/10421; National Academies of Sciences, Engineering, and Medicine, *How People Learn II: Learners, Contexts, and Cultures* (Washington, DC: National Academies Press, 2018), https://doi.org/10.17226/24783.

25. Julio Cammarota and Michelle Fine, *Revolutionizing Education: Youth Participatory Action Research in Motion* (New York: Routledge, 2008).

26. Mirra, Garcia, and Morrell, *Doing Youth Participatory Action Research.* Emily J. Ozer, "Youth-Led Participatory Action Research: Overview and Potential for Enhancing Adolescent Development," *Child Development Perspectives* 11, no. 3 (2017): 173–77, https://doi.org/10.1111/cdep.12228.

27. Sara Bragg, "'But I Listen to Children Anyway!'—Teacher Perspectives on Pupil Voice," *Educational Action Research* 15, no. 4 (November 2007): 505–18, https://doi.org/10.1080/09650790701663973; Jerusha O. Conner, C. Nathan Ober, and Amanda S. Brown, "The Politics of Paternalism: Adult and Youth Perspectives on Youth Voice in Public Policy," *Teachers College Record* 118, no. 8 (August 2016): 1–48, https://doi.org/10.1177/016146811611800805; Regina Day Langhout and Elizabeth Thomas, "Imagining Participatory Action Research in Collaboration with Children: An Introduction," *American Journal of Community Psychology* 46, no. 1–2 (September 2010): 60–66, https://doi.org/10.1007/s10464-010-9321-1.

28. Jerome Bruner, *The Process of Education* (Cambridge, MA: Harvard University Press, 1960).

29. "Standards in Your State," Common Core State Standards Initiative, https://www.thecorestandards.org/standards-in-your-state/.

30. Carl Bereiter and Marlene Scardamalia, "Education for the Knowledge Age: Design-Centered Models of Teaching and Instruction," in *Handbook of Educational Psychology*, 2nd ed., ed. Patricia A. Alexander and Philip H. Winne (New York: Routledge, 2006): 695–713; Common Core State Standards Initiative, *Common Core State Standards for English Language Arts and Literacy in History/Social Studies, Science, and Technical Subjects*, http://www.thecorestandards.org/assets/CCSSI_ELA%20Standards.pdf; Mariah Kornbluh et al., "Youth Participatory Action Research as an Approach to Sociopolitical Development and the New Academic Standards: Considerations for Educators," *Urban Review* 47, no. 5 (December 2015): 868–92, https://doi.org/10.1007/s11256-015-0337-6.

31. Paulo Freire, "The Importance of the Act of Reading," *Journal of Education* 165, no. 1 (Winter 1983): 5.

32. Mirra, Garcia, and Morrell, *Doing Youth Participatory Action Research*; Caraballo, "YPAR and Critical Epistemologies."
33. Caraballo, "YPAR and Critical Epistemologies."
34. El-Amin et al., "Critical Consciousness"; Jason Irizarry, "Buscando la Libertad: Latino Youths in Search of Freedom in School," *Democracy and Education* 19, no. 1, article 4 (2011), https://democracy educationjournal.org/home/vol19/iss1/4; Seider and Graves, *Schooling for Critical Consciousness*.
35. Morales-Doyle and Frausto, "Youth Participatory Science."
36. Learning in Places Collaborative, Learning in Places website, https://learninginplaces.org.
37. See the resources listed in enote 21.
38. National Research Council, *A Framework for K-12 Science Education: Practices, Crosscutting Concepts, and Core Ideas* (Washington, DC: National Academies Press, 2012), https://doi.org/10.17226/13165.
39. Denise Clark Pope, *Doing School: How We Are Creating a Generation of Stressed-Out, Materialistic, and Miseducated Students* (New Haven, CT: Yale University Press, 2003).
40. Beverly Daniel Tatum, *Can We Talk About Race?: And Other Conversations in an Era of School Resegregation* (Boston: Beacon Press, 2007).
41. Ann Jaquith and Molly B. Zielezinski, *Evaluating Deeper Learning: Retrospect and Prospect*, SCOPE Research Brief (Stanford, CA: Stanford Center for Opportunity Policy in Education, November 21, 2018), 2-5.
42. Carlos P. Hipolito-Delgado et al., "Transformative Student Voice for Sociopolitical Development: Developing Youth of Color as Political Actors," *Research on Adolescence* 32, no. 3 (September 2022): 1098-1108, https://doi.org/10.1111/jora.12753; Carlos P. Hipolito-Delgado et al., "Beyond the Trifold in Civics Presentations: The Measure of Youth Policy Arguments," *Journal of Youth Development* 16, no. 4 (September 2021): 149-165, https://doi.org/10.5195/jyd.2021.1011; Beatriz Salazar and Carlos P. Hipolito-Delgado, "Productive Failure and Sociopolitical Development in Young Black, Indigenous, and People of Color Femmes" (paper presentation, American Educational Research Association Annual Meeting, San Diego, CA, April 21, 2022).
43. Beatriz Salazar et al., "Letting Go: The Importance of Allowing Students to Fail Forward" (presentation and workshop, All-In: Co-Creating Knowledge for Justice Conference, Santa Cruz, CA, October 28, 2022).

Chapter 6

1. William R. Penuel and Daniel J. Gallagher, *Creating Research-Practice Partnerships in Education* (Cambridge, MA: Harvard Education Press, 2017).
2. "Title I," US Department of Education, https://www.ed.gov/laws-and -policy/laws-preschool-grade-12-education/title-I.
3. "Supporting Effective Instruction State Grants (Title II, Part A)," US Department of Education, https://www.ed.gov/grants-and-programs /formula-grants/school-improvement/supporting-effective -instruction-state-grantstitle-ii-part-a.
4. "English Language Acquisition State Grants; Title III, Part A," US Department of Education, https://www.ed.gov/grants-and-programs /formula-grants/formula-grants-special-populations/english -language-acquisition-state-grants-mdash-title-iii-part-a.
5. "Student Support and Academic Enrichment Program (Title IV, Part A)," US Department of Education, https://www.ed.gov/grants -and-programs/formula-grants/school-improvement/student -support-and-academic-enrichment-program.
6. Shelley Zion, Adam York, and Dane Stickney, "Bound Together: White Teachers/Latinx Students Revising Resistance," in *The Power of Resistance: Culture, Ideology and Social Reproduction in Global Contexts*, ed. Rowhea M. Elmesky, Carol Camp Yeakey, and Olivia Marcucci (Bingley, UK: Emerald Publishing, 2017), 429–58.
7. Zion, York, and Stickney, "Bound Together," 456.
8. Anna Betts, "University of Florida Eliminates All D.E.I.-Related Positions," *New York Times*, March 2, 2024, https://www.nytimes.com /2024/03/02/us/university-florida-dei.html; Kiara Alfonseca, "Map: The Impact of Anti-DEI Legislation," ABC News, April 5, 2024, https:// abcnews.go.com/US/map-impact-anti-dei-legislation/story?id =108795967.
9. "Educator Resources," SPLC Learning for Justice, accessed July 3, 2024, https://www.learningforjustice.org/classroom-resources.

Chapter 7

1. Shelley Zion, "Transformative Student Voice: Extending the Role of Youth in Addressing Systemic Marginalization in U.S. Schools," *Multiple Voices: Disability, Race, and Language Intersections in Special Education* 20, no. 1 (Spring 2020): 32–43, https://doi.org/10.56829 /2158-396X-20.1.32.

2. Jesica Siham Fernández, Ben Kirshner, and Deana G. Lewis, "Strategies for Systemic Change: Youth Community Organizing to Disrupt the School-to-Prison Nexus," in *Contemporary Youth Activism: Advancing Social Justice in the United States*, ed. Jerusha Conner and Sonia M. Rosen (Santa Barbara, CA: Praeger, 2016), 93–112; Mark R. Warren, *Willful Defiance: The Movement to Dismantle the School-to-Prison Pipeline* (New York: Oxford University Press, 2022).

3. Shelley Zion et al., "Urban Schooling and the Transformative Possibilities of Participatory Action Research: The Role of Youth in Struggles for Urban Education Justice," in *Handbook of Urban Education*, 2nd ed., ed. H. Richard Milner IV and Kofi Lomotey (New York: Routledge, 2021), 507–22.

4. Susan W. Woolley, "GSAs (Gay-Straight Alliances or Gender-Sexuality Alliances)," in *Encyclopedia of Queer Studies in Education*, ed. Kamden K. Strunk and Stephanie Ann Shelton (Leiden, Netherlands: Brill, 2021), 232–37.

5. Ethan Chang and Rebeca Gamez, "Education Leadership as Accompaniment: From Managing to Cultivating Youth Activism," *Teachers College Record* 124, no. 9 (September 1, 2022): 65–90, https://doi.org/10.1177/01614681221129401.

6. Henry Jenkins et al., *By Any Media Necessary: The New Youth Activism* (New York: New York University Press, 2016); Tafadzwa Tivaringe and Ben Kirshner, "Youth Activism in Postapartheid South Africa," in *The Cambridge Handbook of Community Empowerment*, ed. Brian Christens (Cambridge: Cambridge University Press, 2024); Adam Smidi and Saif Shahin, "Social Media and Social Mobilisation in the Middle East: A Survey of Research on the Arab Spring," *India Quarterly* 73, no. 2 (June 2017): 196–209, https://doi.org/10.1177/0974928417700798.

7. Dane Stickney and Julissa Ventura, "Students and Teachers United: Line-Stepping into the Public Political Sphere" (unpublished manuscript, 2023).

8. Daniel J. Losen and Paul Martinez, "Is California Doing Enough to Close the School Discipline Gap?," *Civil Rights Project*, June 21, 2020, https://www.civilrightsproject.ucla.edu/research/k-12-education/school-discipline/is-california-doing-enough-to-close-the-school-discipline-gap.

9. Tracey L. Shollenberger, "Racial Disparities in School Suspension and Subsequent Outcomes: Evidence from the National Longitudinal Survey of Youth," in *Closing the School Discipline Gap: Equitable Remedies*

for Excessive Exclusion, ed. Daniel J. Losen (New York: Teachers College Press, 2015), 31–43.

10. Warren, *Willful Defiance*.

11. Fernández, Kirshner, and Lewis, "Strategies for Systemic Change."

12. Published reports about these outcomes are not cited so as to protect the anonymity of the partnership.

13. Ben Kirshner, *Youth Activism in an Era of Education Inequality* (New York: New York University Press, 2015).

14. Shepherd Zeldin, Linda Camino, and Matthew Calvert, "Toward an Understanding of Youth in Community Governance: Policy Priorities and Research Directions," *Social Policy Report* 17, no. 3 (Autumn 2003): 1–20.

15. Chang and Gamez, "Education Leadership as Accompaniment."

Chapter 8

1. Patricia Hill Collins, *Black Feminist Thought: Knowledge, Consciousness, and the Politics of Empowerment* (New York: Routledge, 1991).

2. Dane Stickney et al., *Transformative Student Voice for Teachers: A Guide to Classroom Action* (Cambridge, MA: Harvard Education Press, forthcoming 2025).

3. Nolan L. Cabrera et al., "Missing the (Student Achievement) Forest for All the (Political) Trees: Empiricism and the Mexican American Studies Controversy in Tucson," *American Educational Research Journal* 51, no. 6 (December 2014): 1084–1118, https://doi.org/10.3102/0002831214553705; Dana L. Mitra, "Amplifying Student Voice," *Educational Leadership* 66, no. 3 (November 2008): 20–25.

4. Grant Wiggins, "The Case for Authentic Assessment," *Practical Assessment, Research and Evaluation* 2, no. 2 (November 1990): 1–4, https://doi.org/10.7275/ffb1-mm19.

5. Ben Kirshner et al., "The Measure of Youth Policy Arguments: An Approach to Supporting Democratic Participation and Student Voice," *Democracy and Education* 28, no. 2, article 4 (December 2020), https://democracyeducationjournal.org/home/vol28/iss2/4/.

Appendix A

1. National Research Council, *Engaging Schools: Fostering High School Students' Motivation to Learn* (Washington, DC: National Academies Press, 2004), https://doi.org/10.17226/10421; National Academies of Sciences, Engineering, and Medicine, *How People Learn II: Learners, Contexts, and Cultures* (Washington, DC: National Academies Press, 2018), https://doi.org/10.17226/24783.

2. Deanna Kuhn and Sam Franklin, "The Second Decade: What Develops (and How)," in *Handbook of Child Psychology: Cognition, Perception, and Language,* 6th ed., ed. William Damon et al. (Hoboken, NJ: John Wiley and Sons, 2006), 953–93; Reed Larson and David Hansen, "The Development of Strategic Thinking: Learning to Impact Human Systems in a Youth Activism Program," *Human Development* 48, no. 6 (November–December 2005): 327–49, https://doi.org/10.1159/000088251.

3. Adena M. Klem and James P. Connell, "Relationships Matter: Linking Teacher Support to Student Engagement and Achievement," *Journal of School Health* 74, no. 7 (September 2004): 262–73, https://doi.org/10.1111/j.1746-1561.2004.tb08283.x.

4. Joseph Kahne et al., "Is Responsiveness to Student Voice Related to Academic Outcomes? Strengthening the Rationale for Student Voice in School Reform," *American Journal of Education* 128, no. 3 (May 2022): 389–415, https://doi.org/10.1086/719121.

5. Nolan L. Cabrera et al., "Missing the (Student Achievement) Forest for All the (Political) Trees: Empiricism and the Mexican American Studies Controversy in Tucson," *American Educational Research Journal* 51, no. 6 (December 2014): 1084–1118, https://doi.org/10.3102/0002831214553705.

6. Dana L. Mitra, "Student Voice and Student Roles in Education Policy and Policy Reform," in *AERA Handbook of Education Policy Research*, ed. Gary Sykes, Barbara Schneider, and David N. Plank (New York: Routledge, 2009); Jerusha Osberg, Denise Pope, and Mollie Galloway, "Students Matter in School Reform: Leaving Fingerprints and Becoming Leaders," *International Journal of Leadership in Education* 9, no. 4 (November 2006): 329–43, https://doi.org/10.1080/13603120600895338.

7. Carlos P. Hipolito-Delgado and Shelley Zion, "Igniting the Fire Within Marginalized Youth: The Role of Critical Civic Inquiry in Fostering Ethnic Identity and Civic Self-Efficacy," *Urban Education* 52, no. 6 (July 2017): 699–717, https://doi.org/10.1177/0042085915574524; Julio Cammarota, "A Social Justice Approach to Achievement: Guiding Latina/o Students Toward Educational Attainment with a Challenging, Socially Relevant Curriculum," *Equity and Excellence in Education* 40, no. 1 (February 2007): 87–96, https://doi.org/10.1080/10665680601015153.

8. Scott Seider and Daren Graves, *Schooling for Critical Consciousness: Engaging Black and Latinx Youth in Analyzing, Navigating, and Challenging Racial Injustice* (Cambridge, MA: Harvard Education Press, 2020).

9. Cathy Cohen, Joseph Kahne, and Jessica Marshall, *Let's Go There: Race, Ethnicity, and a Lived Civics Approach to Civic Education* (Chicago: University of Chicago Press, 2018), https://www.civicsurvey.org/publications/lets-go-there.

10. Jerusha Conner, Michael Posner, and Bright Nsowaa, "The Relationship Between Student Voice and Student Engagement in Urban High Schools," *Urban Review* 54 (December 2022): 755–74, https://doi.org/10.1007/s11256-022-00637-2; Jerusha Conner et al., "Student Voice and Choice in the Classroom: Promoting Academic Engagement," in *Instructional Strategies for Active Learning*, ed. Kira Carbonneau (InTechOpen, 2024), https://doi.org/10.5772/intechopen.114346.

11. "Elevate Student Voice," The CASEL Guide to Schoolwide Social and Emotional Learning, https://schoolguide.casel.org/focus-area-3/school/elevate-student-voice/; Ursula Mager and Peter Nowak, "Effects of Student Participation in Decision Making at School: A Systematic Review and Synthesis of Empirical Research," *Educational Research Review* 7, no. 1 (January, 2012): 38–61, https://doi.org/10.1016/j.edurev.2011.11.001.

12. Carlos P. Hipolito-Delgado et al., "Transformative Student Voice for Sociopolitical Development: Developing Youth of Color as Political Actors," *Research on Adolescence* 32, no. 3 (September 2022): 1098–1108, https://doi.org/10.1111/jora.12753; Emily J. Ozer and Laura Douglas, "The Impact of Participatory Research on Urban Teens: An Experimental Evaluation," *American Journal of Community Psychology* 51, no. 1–2 (2013): 66–75, https://doi.org/10.1007/s10464-012-9546-2.

13. Eric Toshalis and Michael J. Nakkula, *Motivation, Engagement, and Student Voice*, Students at the Center Series (Boston: Jobs for the Future, April 2012), https://www.howyouthlearn.org/pdf/Motivation%20Engagement%20Student%20Voice_0.pdf; Susan Yonezawa and Makeba Jones, "Using Students' Voices to Inform and Evaluate Secondary School Reform," in *International Handbook of Student Experience in Elementary and Secondary School*, ed. Dennis Thiessen and Alison Cook-Sather (Dordrecht, Netherlands: Springer, 2007), 681–709; Mitra, "Student Voice and Student Roles."

14. Emily J. Ozer, "Youth-Led Participatory Action Research: Overview and Potential for Enhancing Adolescent Development," *Child Development Perspectives* 11, no. 3 (2017): 173–77, https://doi.org/10.1111/cdep.12228.

15. Jerusha Conner, Samantha Holquist, Dana Mitra, and Search Institute, State of Student Voices in Schools Survey, (Minneapolis: Search Institute, 2023); https://searchinstitute.org/resources-hub/state-of -student-voice-practices-in-schools-survey; Jerusha Conner et al., "Measuring Student Voice Practices: The Development and Validation of School and Classroom Scales," AERA Open (2025).

Appendix B

1. Paulo Freire, *Pedagogy of the Oppressed,* 30th Anniversary ed. (New York: Continuum, 2000), 34.

2. Deborah Roseman (@roseperson), "This quote about respect isn't 100% applicable to the trending topic of the day, yet I can't stop thinking about it. HT stimmyabby.tumblr.com," X post and photo, August 27, 2019, https://x.com/roseperson/status/1166359853960499201.

3. Anna Nichols, "Help! My Students Are Talking Back!," *Managing the Art Classroom* (blog), undated, https://artteachershelpal.blogspot.com /p/help-my-students-are-talking-back.html.

Acknowledgments

We would like to thank the following people who have played critical roles as researchers and educators with the TSV research group over the last fifteen years:

Adam York, Beatrice Carey Carter, Beatriz Salazar, Bill Rozycki, Carrie Allen, Charles Barnes, Dan Tulino, Daniela DiGiacomo, Elizabeth Mendoza, Erik Dutilly, Erin Allaman, Eshe Price, Ginnie Logan, Jaime Ramge, Janelle Alexander, Jessica Neuman, Joanna Mendy, Jordana Simmons, Julissa Ventura, Kareem Kalil, Laura-Elena Porras Holguin, Lorena Silva de Andrade Dias, Melissa Campanella, Mónica González Ybarra, Montserrat Estrada Martin, Nina Walker, Rita Tracy, Scott Oswald, Sharada Krishnamurthy, and Solicia Lopez.

A special thank you to Dane Stickney. You are instrumental to the team; your knowledge on teacher training, contributions to curriculum development, enthusiasm for writing, and commitment to elevating student voice have all been critical to advancing TSV. We can't imagine doing this work without you!

While our IRB protocols require that we maintain the anonymity of the districts, schools, community organizations, educators, and students with whom we've worked, know that we see you. You allowed us into your classrooms and meetings, you shared your personal stories, hopes, and fears. Thank you for trusting us to tell these stories. You inspire us personally and professionally. Our work is richer because of your dedication.

We also acknowledge each other. We started this endeavor as three untenured faculty, in different disciplines, from different race/gender/class/religious backgrounds, with different communication (and conflict!) styles—and we stayed in it. Through tenure and promotions, relocations, family joys and pains—we navigated our identities and commitments, had challenging conversations, and built an amazing team that models the values we stand for—sharing power and voice, developing critical consciousness, and taking action.

Research reported in this book took place over many years and was supported at different times with grants from the following entities: the Spencer Foundation, the Hewlett Foundation, the William T. Grant Foundation, the American Educational Research Association, KnowledgeWorks, and the US Department of Education. The views expressed are those of the authors and do not necessarily reflect the views of the research funders.

About the Authors

SHELLEY, BEN, AND CARLOS have been working together since 2008, developing the ideas shared here—and found on their website, www.transformativestudentvoice.net.

SHELLEY ZION is a professor of urban education at Rowan University, and principal investigator of the PEER (Partnerships for Educational Equity and Research) lab. In this role, she coaches leaders and leads training, research, and community partnerships focused on issues of access, success, and equity. Shelley's team seeks to understand how institutions, social systems, and individual experiences create and sustain systems of power and privilege that ensure access for some while excluding others. Her research is situated within a framework of sociopolitical development, informed by a range of critical theoretical perspectives, and advanced by an understanding of the nature of both individual and systemic change. This framework requires that to impact a transformation of the current public education and other social systems toward goals of equity and social justice, we must work to disrupt dominant ideologies by creating spaces in which people begin to develop a critical understanding of the cultural, political, economic, and other institutional forces that perpetuate systems of privilege and oppression. We must work to develop a critical consciousness, reflective practice, and commitment to action in relation to institutional structures, policies, and practices and transform those systems toward healing historical wounds, dismantling oppressive systems, and creating equitable access to opportunity. This work requires that education leaders, faculty, staff, community members and students come together to design new ways of thinking about public school.

BEN KIRSHNER is a professor of learning sciences and human development at the University of Colorado Boulder. His experiences working with young people at a community center in San Francisco's Mission District motivated his research agenda focused on young people's critical consciousness and their roles leading social justice change. Ben works collaboratively with educators, community organizers, graduate students, and youth to design and study learning environments that support youth development, activism, and civic participation. In his work with the Transformative Student Voice research group (along with Shelley Zion and Carlos Hipolito-Delgado), Ben develops research-practice partnerships that increase public schools' capacity to support student voice and agency through teacher professional learning, policy alignment, and improvement research. With the Research Hub for Youth Organizing he codesigns educational tools and research studies with youth organizing groups and networks that build capacity for young people to influence policy and public narratives (www.colorado.edu/education-research-hub). His book, *Youth Activism in an Era of Education Inequality*, received the Social Policy award for best authored book from the Society for Research on Adolescence. Ben has also published in journals that include *Journal of the Learning Sciences, Journal of Research on Adolescence, Applied Developmental Science, Journal of Community Psychology,* and *Cognition and Instruction.*

CARLOS P. HIPOLITO-DELGADO is a professor in counseling at the University of Colorado Denver. His research focuses on the sociopolitical development of students of color, the ethnic identity development of Chicane/x and Latine/x youth, and the cultural competence of counselors. He has been co-principal investigator on grants from the Spencer Foundation, the Hewlett Foundation, KnowledgeWorks, and the American Educational Research Association—all focusing on the sociopolitical development of youth and Transformative Student Voice. Through this grant work he has collaborated on the development of assessments of the quality of youth civic performances and the impact of civics curriculum on academic engagement, civic engagement, and sociopolitical development. He has also published on the use of empowerment and sociopolitical development to foster academic engagement and promote educational reform for marginalized communities. He is past president of the Association for Multicultural Counseling and Development (AMCD) and past chair of the American Counseling Association Foundation. He has been recognized with the Exemplary Diversity Leadership award by AMCD and the University of Colorado Denver Faculty Assembly Excellence in Leadership and Service award.

Index

accountings, 99

action civics, 122. *See also* Critical
Civic Inquiry (CCI)

acts of vulnerability, 110–111

adultism, 47, 48, 85–86

advisor student role, 51–53, 60–63

afterschool clubs and activities
case studies, 132–141
challenges for, 142–143
designing own, 135–139
overview, 131–132, 141–142,
150

age segregation, 20, 48

agreements for groups, 45–46,
112–113

agreements for partnerships,
167–168

allies, 41, 56

assessments, 127–128, 134–135,
185–190

audits, 99

authentic assessment, 186–188

Bánáthy, Béla, 10

belonging, 111, 114–115

Blackwell, Meadow, 15, 89–90

blind spots in hallways, 77

break room, 137–138

Bronsen, Jack, 162, 163, 168

Brown, Peter, 99

budget. *See* funding

buy-in, 41–42, 98–99, 147–148

Cammarota, Julio, 116

Campbell, Tania, 114

change, resistance to, 125–127,
180

civic learning, 77, 97. *See also*
Critical Civic Inquiry (CCI)

classrooms. *See* TSV in the
classroom

classrooms, plus delta process in,
109

clubs. *See* afterschool clubs and
activities

collaborator student role, 52, 53,
57–60

Common Core State Standards,
121

communication plans, 41–42

community organizations.
See district-community
partnerships; student
activism

community rituals, 111–112

conflicts, anticipation of, 95–96

consensus-based decision-making model, 45
continuity needs, 97
creative spaces for teachers, 145–146
Critical Civic Inquiry (CCI)
   benefits of, 26–27, 171–172
   in classroom, 119–124
   overview, 12–13
   as protective factor, 26
critical consciousness, 11, 12, 113–114, 176–177
critical conversations tier, 113–119, 124
critical social theory, 113
culture change. *See* mindsets
curriculum, 37, 60, 109, 120.
   See also TSV in the classroom

data gathering and use
   getting started in, 64
   professional development based on, 58
   root cause of problem, identification of, 18
   student learning from doing, 162, 169
   vertical integration and, 39
decision-making protocols, 44–45, 112
defensiveness of critiques, 95–96
deficit narratives, 126
DeMeulenaere, Eric, 111–112
democratic participation, 77
discipline disparities, 156, 157, 160–164
district-community partnerships, 152, 160–164, 167–168, 184–185

district-level TSV
   barriers to, 31
   benefits of, 174–175
   buy-in and, 98–99
   challenges for, 84–90
   example of, 75–77
   overview, 77, 100–101
   power of, 77–79
   relationship building and, 76, 79–84, 86
   success, tips for, 90–98
   vertical integration and, 29
district mission statements, 5–6, 8
District Summit, 75–76
diversity, equity, and inclusion, dismantling of, 146
diversity of student participants, 68–69, 84–85, 177–179
dress code, 138

elevator pitches, 40, 42
emotional support for teachers, 146–147
equity council, membership of, 54–57, 63–64, 165
ethic of care, 111
exclusion, 114–115

faculty meetings, 150
five-year plan development, 64
Freire, Paulo, 9–10, 11, 113, 121
funding
   afterschool or summer programs, 135–139, 142–143
   commitment and, 99
   grant funding, 82–83, 134, 135–137

importance of, 67, 80–82
Title funds, 135–136

Garces, Antonio, 120–121
Gianelli, Sofia, 36
GirlsInTech program,
    132–133
Girls LEAD, 139
goals, for engaging student
    voice, 64
grants. *See* funding
grassroot organizations.
    See district-community
    partnerships; student activism

Harris, Ann, 136–137
Heart-Mind Online, 46
hierarchies of power, 85–86
high-achieving students, 84–85,
    177
hiring, student voice in, 34,
    59–60
horizontal integration of TSV, 28,
    34, 35, 79, 180–181
humanities, 115–116, 121–123

identity, 23, 97, 116
immigration rights, 104–106
implementation monitoring,
    168–169
implementation timelines,
    67–68
injustice, as human-made, 11
interest alignment, 88–89, 179

Jones, Brook, 139–140

leader as decision-makers, 44
leader student role, 52, 53–57
LGBTQIA+ students, 154, 165
listening, 95–96
local versus national group
    activism, 164–165
lone wolves concept, 145–146

majority rule, 45
marginalized backgrounds,
    students with
    insights from, 78–79, 175
    outcomes from TSV for,
        97, 176
    using science to transform
        communities, 118
Measure of Youth Policy
    Arguments (MYPA), 187
meetings, team, 43–46
meetings, agreements for,
    45–46
mentors, 93–95
metal detector installation, 159
microaggressions, student
    collaborators and,
    57–59
Migrant Youth Leadership
    Institute, 138
mindsets
    adultism, 47, 48, 85–86
    professional development to
        shift, 144–148
    for TSV, 20–25
mission statements, 5–6, 8
Morales-Doyle, Daniel,
    117–118
motivations for TSV, 40
MYPA (Measure of Youth Policy
    Arguments), 187

national versus local group
    activism, 164–165
Next Generation Science
    Standards, 117
norms for meetings, 45

O'Neil, Edward, 30, 49–50
organization chart creation, 41
Overton, Sean, 24–25, 135

partnerships. *See also* youth-adult
    partnerships
    district-community
        partnerships, 152, 160–164,
        167–168, 184–185
    research-practice partnership
        (RPP), 82–83, 134–135,
        184–185
perceptions, student voice to
    change, 55–56
planning for TSV
    barriers in, 47–49
    five-year plan development, 64
    foundations needed, 63–64
    goals of, 33–34, 64
    horizontal integration and,
        34, 35
    laying the groundwork, 39–42
    resources needed, 67
    structures, creation of, 46–47
    team building, 42–46
    timelines for implementation,
        67–68
plus delta process, 60, 109
Poder Comunitario-district
    partnership, 152, 160–164
police officers in schools, 55,
    160

policies and practices, 19–20,
    87–88, 99
political action, 97
political support for teachers,
    146–147
Positive Behavior Interventions
    and Supports (PBIS), 61
power, asymmetry in, 166–167
power sharing, 85–86, 107–113,
    124, 184
PRIDE club, 139
Pritchard, Jen, 115
problems, action to address as
    key element of TSV, 18–19
"problem" students, engagement
    of, 178–179
professional development
    importance of, 67, 94–95,
        143–144, 182–183
    project management skills,
        148–150
    student-led, 58, 147–148
    timelines for implementation
        and, 67–68
    transformational adult
        learning, 144–148
    vertical integration and, 37
project-based learning, benefits
    of, 127
project management skills,
    148–150
protests. *See* student activism

REDI agreements, 46, 57
relationship building, 76, 79–84,
    86
research-practice partnership
    (RPP), 82–83, 134–135,
    184–185

resistance to change, 125–127, 180

resources, lack of, 49, 67, 68. *See also* funding

right-wing activism, 164–165

rituals, 111–112

root cause, identification of, 18, 114

rubrics, 65–66, 188

scheduling challenges, 38–39, 48, 132, 142–143

school boards, 29, 60–61, 87, 158–160

school climate, student voice in, 60–63

school closure study, 166–167

school mission statements, 5–6, 8

school reform and improvement versus school transformation, 7–10

school resource officers (SROs), 55, 160

schools, barriers to TSV for, 31

schools, benefits of TSV for, 174–175

school-to-prison pipeline, 160

shared power, 85–86, 107–113, 124

shared responsibility, 109–110, 144–145

small groups, 127

social media use, 155–157

sociopolitical development (SPD), 22–23, 26

soft skills, importance of, 140–141

Sosa, Mercedes, 8, 47

stamina, 49

standardized assessment, 186–187

STEM, 117–119, 123–124

structural segregation, 20, 48–49

student activism
    critical consciousness and, 177
    defined, 151
    lessons about, 164–169
    as opportunity, 151–152
    overview, 153–155, 169–170
    proactive approaches to, 160–164, 170
    reactive approaches to, 155–160
    reasons for, 155

Student Break Center, 137–138

student engagement. *See also* Critical Civic Inquiry (CCI); youth-adult partnerships
    as benefit of TSV, 175–176, 189
    benefits of, 85
    creating space for, 10, 173
    critical consciousness and, 12
    critical conversations and, 118
    of "problem" students, 178–179
    student voice to increase, 14

student-led movements, TSV compared, 22. *See also* student activism

students
    benefits of TSV for, 128–129
    centering of, 24
    leadership roles for, 109–110
    resistance to change, 125–126, 180

student-teacher relationship, importance of, 107–108

student voice
    advisor role, 51–53, 60–63
    collaborator role, 52, 53, 57–60

student voice, *continued*
  contradiction between rhetoric
    and reality, 6-7, 36
  in decision-making, 46-47
  foundations for, 63-64
  goals setting about, 64
  interest alignment and, 88-89,
    179
  leader role, 52, 53-57
  as not enough for TSV, 25
  personal opinions versus
    representative opinions, 57
  "preparedness" for, 47
  rubric for, 65-66
  student feedback, 24-25, 52-53
  symbolic voice, 86-88, 179
student voice office/leader
  choice of, 46, 93, 96
  cohesion provided by, 91-92
  importance of, 100, 181-182
  success of program due to,
    76-77
  vertical integration of TSV
    and, 29
Student Voice Summit, 75
student voice teams, 15
summer sessions
  case studies, 132-141
  challenges for, 142-143
  designing own, 135-139
  overview, 131, 141-142, 150
superintendents, 29, 60-61,
    80-82
support
  emotional and political,
    146-147
  importance of, 67
  for students, 190
  from superintendents, 80-82
  for TSV leaders, 183

sustained and systemic
  opportunities, as key
  element of TSV, 17-18
symbolic voice, 86-88, 179
system change versus system
  maintenance, 10-11
systems change, 8, 10-11, 13, 28
systems design, as mindset,
    23-24

teachers. *See also* professional
    development
  acts of vulnerability by, 110-111
  barriers to TSV for, 30
  benefits of TSV for, 129,
    174-175
  demographics of compared to
    students, 14
  impacts of, 171
  resistance to change, 125, 180
team building, 42-46
team meetings, 43-46
testimonials, 189-190
tiers. *See* TSV in the classroom
time needs, 48, 67, 96-98, 143
Title funds, 135-136
transformational adult learning,
    144-148
Transformative Student Voice
    (TSV). *See also* afterschool
    clubs and activities; district-
    level TSV; planning for TSV;
    summer sessions; TSV in the
    classroom
  assessments of impact of,
    127-128, 134-135, 185-190
  barriers to, 29-31
  benefits of, 172-173, 174-177
  CCI as foundation of, 12-14

challenges for, 177–181
defined, 15–17
effectiveness of, 25–27, 85
horizontal integration and, 28,
180–181
key elements of, 17–20,
181–185, 190
key takeaways about, 173–181
mindsets for, 20–25
need for, 5–7
vertical integration of, 27–29
what is not, 25
why use, 14–15
transportation, 48–49, 142
trust
acts of vulnerability and,
110–111
importance of, 107–108
student activism and, 166–168
in youth-adult partnerships,
22, 24–25, 29–30, 50, 85–86
TSV in the classroom
benefits of, 128–129
challenges for, 124–128
Critical Civic Inquiry and,
119–124
critical conversations tier,
113–119, 124
example of, 104–106
overview, 103–104, 124
power sharing tier, 107–113,
124, 184

undocumented students,
college access for,
105–106, 171–172

vertical integration of TSV,
27–29, 34, 36–39. *See also*
district-level TSV
violations of meeting agreements,
46
visionary pragmatism, 9, 174
vulnerability, acts of, 110–111

walkouts, 156, 157–158
Watts, Roderick, 22
wellness room, 137–138
White, Derek, 43, 78, 108–109,
149
Witte, Malcolm, 140–141

youth-adult partnerships
defined, 21
diversity in, 68–69
guidelines for, 168–169
as key element of TSV, 19,
183–184
as mindset, 20–22
trust and, 22, 24–25, 29–30,
50, 85–86
Youth Leaders (YL) program,
75–77, 81, 187. *See also*
district-level TSV
Youth Participatory Action
Research (YPAR), 11–12, 119,
121, 127. *See also* Critical
Civic Inquiry (CCI)

zero tolerance rules, 160. *See also*
discipline disparities